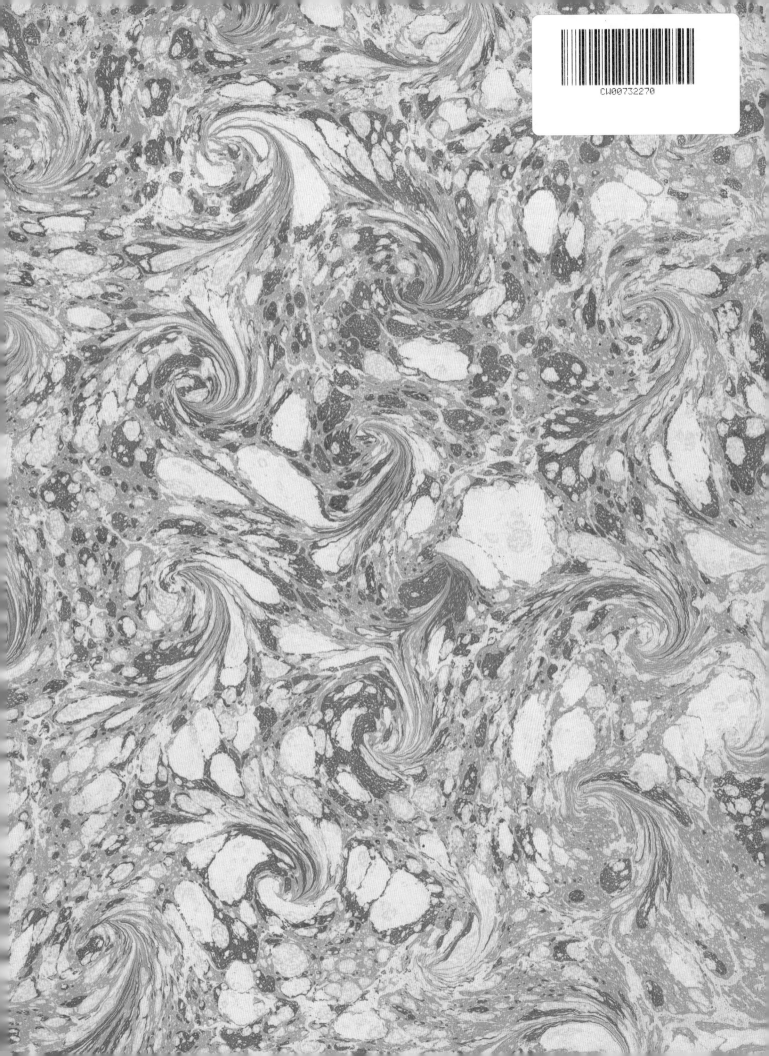

The German National Railway

The German National Railway

in World War II

Janusz Piekalkiewicz

Schiffer Military History
Atglen, PA

Book translation by Dr. Edward Force, Central Connecticut State

Book Design by Ian Robertson.

Copyright © 2008 by Schiffer Publishing.
Library of Congress Control Number: 2008929532

Printed in China.
ISBN: 978-0-7643-3097-1

This book was originally published in German under the title
Die Deutsche Reichsbahn im Zweiten Weltkrieg by Motorbuch Verlag

We are interested in hearing from authors with book ideas on related topics.

Published by Schiffer Publishing Ltd.
4880 Lower Valley Road
Atglen, PA 19310
Phone: (610) 593-1777
FAX: (610) 593-2002
E-mail: Info@schifferbooks.com.
Visit our web site at: www.schifferbooks.com
Please write for a free catalog.
This book may be purchased from the publisher.
Please include $5.00 postage.
Try your bookstore first.

In Europe, Schiffer books are distributed by:
Bushwood Books
6 Marksbury Avenue
Kew Gardens
Surrey TW9 4JF, England
Phone: 44 (0) 20 8392-8585
FAX: 44 (0) 20 8392-9876
E-mail: Info@bushwoodbooks.co.uk.
Visit our website at: www.bushwoodbooks.co.uk
Free postage in the UK. Europe: air mail at cost.
Try your bookstore first.

Contents

Foreword

The tasks of the German *Reichsbahn* of carrying on transport and traffic during World War II were extensive and decisively important. Its history is as manifold as its relations to warfare, armament, and party leadership.

At no time did the German *Reichsbahn* have to overcome greater difficulties; in no period of its existence were more stringent demands made on it and carried out. This had an essential influence on both the course and the extent of the war. But in crass contrast to all three sections of the *Wehrmacht* or the SS, from whose ranks many became acquainted with them for one reason or another, the hundred thousand of their railroad men, in their blue and gray uniforms, remained anonymous to their contemporaries. Even General Gercke, high commander of military transportation, is a very unknown figure to the uninformed. The man who, from the first to the last day of the war, directed a transport system that at times covered all of the continent of Europe except the Iberian peninsula, remains unmentioned in most annals of World War II. A profound memory, which never left him in the lurch, helped him to direct the complicated and ponderous apparatus over Scylla and Charybdis, despite the tremendous burdens placed on it by foe and friend.

Today nobody knows precisely how he succeeded at this enormous accomplishment. Frail, modest, and plagued by fate, Gercke was a true individual among generals, and ordered all his war diaries to be burned shortly after the war ended. And when General Gercke passed away in the hospital of an American prison camp at Marburg on the Lahn in 1946, he took his secrets with him to the grave.

Thus irreplaceable documents were lost with the total collapse of the Reich in 1945, and the most important files with the seal of secrecy were, on command, almost completely destroyed.

The occupying powers added to this misfortune: On the one hand, they confiscated whole truckloads of important files, which vanished once and for all; on the other hand, they saw to it through threats of punishment that numerous documents that still existed here and there were quickly destroyed to avoid personal disadvantage. Similarly, harmless but informative documents, such as factory records and the like, were consigned to paper mills in the first few years for lack of raw materials.

Since leading personalities of the railway system and involved military command are generally no longer among the living, and their reports and statistics, which could not be published then for reasons of secrecy, and could provide important insight into the military capability of the railways or their wartime losses, have for the most part been consigned to the flames, it is a very special undertaking to reconstruct the war history of the German *Reichsbahn* even in fragmentary form.

Janusz Piekalkiewicz

The Chief of Transportation, General of the Infantry Rudolf Gercke

1

"In modern mobile war, tactics are no longer the main thing; the decisive factor is the organization of supplying, so as to maintain the moment of motion."—Thus wrote Liddell Hart, and he was right.

Misled by the initial success of the *Blitzkrieg*, Hitler believed that the motorization of the army overshadowed the significance of the railways in overcoming logistic problems. This false assumption avenged itself tragically, especially in the Russian campaign: only too late did the German command notice that the classical rail lines were the surest and most productive transit routes in this war too. Yet the German railroads that were ignored by Hitler had always ranked among the world's best. At the time when Hitler was formulating his plans of conquest, the German *Reichsbahn* (DRB) was a perfectly directed organization.

At the top was the Reich Traffic Ministry with eight railroad offices. Subordinate to it were three upper operational commands: East in Berlin, South in Munich, and West in Essen. There were also 26 railroad administration offices and, for special tasks, two central railroad offices in Berlin and Munich.

With the takeover of the Austrian railways, four new railroad administrative offices were formed: Innsbruck, Linz, Villach, and Vienna. The railway office in Innsbruck was divided among the bordering German Railways offices in July 1939, as were the Sudeten German offices after that area was absorbed. The Memelland railways were assigned to the RBK office in Koenigsberg, Prussia. The railways in the Protectorate of Bohemia and Moravia took a special position. The Protectorate was autonomous, but the Reich itself oversaw the transport system.

The military interests, aside from the basic matters supervised by the Chief of Transportation, were represented by the General Transport Department, later the *Wehrmacht* Transport Department. Military transport was subordinate to the "Chief of Transportation," General Gercke. He belonged to the General Staff in the Army High Command and was simultaneously "*Wehrmacht* Transport Chief" in the *Wehrmacht* High Command. His service position was similar to that of a "Commanding General." To carry out his tasks in all theaters of war he administered:

1. The field transport department for planning and carrying out the transport of troops and supplies, as well as *Wehrmacht* travel traffic.

2. The planning department for the organization of the transport system, which built and maintained transport routes in Germany and occupied countries.

3. The homeland transport department for all administrative and customs-law matters in the German war zone, and for cooperation with the involved civil ministries.

4. The personnel department for the administration of the employees and troops assigned to the transport system.

5. The information department for the construction and maintenance of the transport system's own communication network and the direction of the involved communication troops.
   In addition, the "Commander of the Railway Engineering Troops" ("Bedeis"), which directed all railway engineering troops and was simultaneously the technical advisor of the "Transport Chief," was also subordinate to him. Departments 4 and 5 were instituted only during the course of World War II.

The duty of the "Chief of Transportation" included both railroads and inland ship transport. The territorial transport offices, in which the transport commands always had a seat in the railroad administration in Germany and occupied countries, were also subordinate. Subordinated to them in turn were railroad officers at major junction depots and "flying" loading and unloading commissioners. As of 1941 these transport commands were united in "Wehrmacht Transport Commands" and Transport Command offices in the large command administrations, such as army groups or armies.

Some 51,010 men were at the disposal of the General of Transport in an Army Group: one railroad engineer brigade with a total of 14,858 men; one railroad communication regiment with 1500 men; one light flak battalion to protect railway transport, with 600 men; one transport security regiment with staff and battalions (8617 men in all); one field railroad battalion with field transport battalions, field machine battalions, and field workshop battalions, plus country rifle battalions with a training battalion (22,112 men in all); and various other battalions.

The railway engineer troops were in charge of the first makeshift repairs of the rail lines and objects during an advance and the establishment of front service. It was their task to destroy railway facilities during a retreat.

The rail network that existed in Germany at the beginning of the war had a length of some 68,000 kilometers. For passenger and freight service there were 12,317 railway system depots and 1,708 depots of private lines available. The rolling stock included some 23,000 locomotives, 1,892 other engines, 69,000 passenger cars, 605,000 freight cars, and 21,000 baggage cars.

But the DRB was allowed to enter World War II insufficiently prepared. In the autumn of 1939 there were, in fact, fewer locomotives than in 1914. This was caused by the concept of full motorization, symbolized by the Reich Autobahn system; personnel and materials were likewise not comparable with the state of armaments in the Reich.

The precise military preparation of the advance against Poland allowed it to run according to plan—aside from some disturbances—although the total number of transport missions was greater than in 1914: on an average, 4,000 trains with 55,000 cars covered 200 kilometers at that time.

The Army High Command absolutely wanted to take control of the only rail connection between East Prussia and the Reich, which ran until then in the so-called "Polish Corridor." The most important and amazing point in this plan, though, was the Vistula bridge at Tczev (Dirschau). If it were blown up, then the problem-free supplying of the Third Army in East Prussia would no longer be possible. As the Chief of the General Staff, General of the Artillery Halder, noted in his diary, it was considered how the Dirschau bridge could be captured by a surprise attack.

The Colonel of the Railway Engineers, Karl Busick, a former Austrian officer, was given the task of scouting the railroad bridge at Tczev and making all preparations for a quick rebuilding of the bridge in case the Polish Army blew it up. On 5 August, Busick could already report the first scouting results that he, as a civilian, had made on his railroad trips over the bridge and through observations with a telescope from the Marienburg highlands by the river. He reported where Polish sentry posts were located, where explosive materials and positions were, how the explosive lines ran and what damage could be caused. Busick suspected, which was later confirmed, that the explosion was to be set off from one small house on the railroad at Tczev. The Austrian then named the positions in which the materials needed for repairs could be stored in the vicinity of the Marienburg depot. Transporting the equipment had to be done under strictest secrecy, since the Polish railroads ran their locomotives as far as the Marienburg depot.

Hitler was informed of the results of the observation and involved Himmler. What great importance this undertaking had to the *Wehrmacht* High Command is shown by "Instruction No. 1 for Waging War" of August 31, 1939, in which Tczev (Dirschau) is mentioned. The order requires that "at the beginning of warfare, the railroad bridge and also the road bridge to the south of it be taken in a surprise attack."

The *Luftwaffe* had orders to prevent Polish soldiers, through rolling action, from destroying the important object. Before that, pinpoint bomb attacks were to destroy the ignition point, the small house spotted by Colonel Busick. First Lieutenant Bruno Dilley, leader of the 3rd detachment of Stuka Squadron 1, and his radioman, Sergeant Hans Kather, were given the order to carry out this mission. It was the first bomb attack of World War II.

The two aviators, disguised as civilians, often crossed the bridge of Tczev on the Koenigsberg-Berlin express train and made sure that the explosive lines ran straight from the ignition point at the depot along the southern slope of the railroad embankment. At the Insterburg airfield they then practiced pinpoint attacks on this small object with their Ju 87 B every day.

Several engineer companies were to be hidden in an empty freight train, which was to be passed off as an empty train of the Polish railroad authority to be picked up at the Marienburg depot. The train crew would then be overpowered and replaced on the return trip by Germans in Polish uniforms. An armored train with an Army battle group, led by Colonel Medem, was to follow shortly after the "empty freight train." The Stuka attack on the Tczev depot was planned for the same moment at which the train approached the railroad bridge. When the train reached the bridge, the engineers were to jump out of the cars, cut the still-undamaged wires to the explosion points that Colonel Busick had spotted, and capture the Polish bridge guards. Since a German express train from Schneidemuehl was to come onto the line at the exact same time as the attack and had to stop at Dirschau, the Transport Command Frankfurt (on the Oder) had the task of delaying the express train in Schneidemuehl until the air raid was finished.

Twenty minutes before the war planned by Hitler began, the three dive-bombers of the 3rd Detachment, under First Lieutenant Dilley, took off from nearby Elbing. In the first morning light of September 1, 1939, they flew low over the fog-shrouded Vistula valley in the direction of the fateful bridge. At 4:34 AM the bombs exploded exactly on their target.

But things did not go as planned. The armored train of Colonel Medem was stopped by the Poles. At 6:30 AM, long before the first German advance reached Tczev, they blew up the bridge which, when built in 1857, was regarded, with its six 131-meter spans over the Vistula and the lowlands, as the most boldly built bridge in the world. Thus, the only railroad connection with East Prussia was broken, and a great part of the supplies had to be sent by roundabout routes on the Baltic Sea.

Opening of express-train traffic from Berlin to East Prussia via Stettin-Danzig-Dirschau to public transport

"From October 2, 1939 on, traffic between East Prussia and the rest of the Reich is established over the following land route: Berlin Stettiner Depot as of 8:40 A.M., Danzig Main Depot at 4:52 P.M., Dirschau at 5:28 P.M. In Dirschau, crossing the Vistula by ferry and then motor bus travel to the Liessau depot are necessary . . . In order to meet the serious need for these trains, the Reichsbahn has decided to run trains before and after these express trains. The passengers need no particular transit pass, but the possession of official photo identification is required. In the formerly Polish area, leaving the train is not allowed. The still existing customs and passport requirements at the border of the former Free State of Danzig remain unaffected by this regulation."

Reichsbahn, 41/1939

Only on October 15, 1939, could a train again cross the bridge at Tczev.

To be sure, the two Vistula bridges in Warsaw were spared by the war's events, but eleven bridges over the Vistula, San, and Bug were already in ruins. Most of the approximately 8000 fully destroyed and 25,000 damaged railroad cars in Poland were struck by the German *Luftwaffe*. Railroad engineers were constantly repairing damaged rail lines, and soldiers were running some partial lines with the help of Polish railroad personnel.

At the beginning of the Polish campaign, the German railroad personnel carried out their first great war achievement: transporting the 86 non-motorized divisions to the eastern and western boundaries of the Reich.

The Polish campaign went quickly, and during the combat the railroad did not play a major role in supplying, but the destruction of the railroad lines reached a hitherto unknown extent.

With mobilization, the German *Reichsbahn* was instructed to introduce the fullest schedules. Public transport was almost completely halted temporarily in the night of August 25-26, 1939.

Poznan becomes Posen

"On Sunday, September 24, 1939 the formal raising of the flag on the railroad administration building in Posen took place. With this symbolic act, the official activity of the first German railroad administration on formerly German soil took place, after a twenty-year Polish interregnum".

Reichsbahn, 41/1939

Hitler also knew how to appreciate the advantages and comfort of the German *Reichsbahn*. On September 3, 1939—France and Britain had just declared war on the Third Reich—the *Führer* and his staff left Berlin and set out for the Polish front. The German *Reichsbahn* made the "Führer's First Headquarters" available. It was a special train with an AA-gun car with 2-cm guns at each end of the train, several cars for communications and the press, a workroom and a salon car for Hitler, sleeping cars for the staff, and a dining car. The rolling headquarters with its highly polished train of cars went first to Bad Polzin, then Gross-Born, and was finally switched to a sidetrack near the depot in Illnau. From there Hitler made his visits to the front in a heavy Mercedes-Benz G 4.

On 16 September, the Führer's special train moved its position to Goddentov-Lanz, near Danzig. The commander of this DRB Führer headquarters was a then very unknown colonel, Erwin Rommel. After three weeks, Hitler started back to Berlin in his "rolling headquarters" on September 26, 1939. Only in April 1941—during the Balkan campaign—did he last use the special *Reichsbahn* train as his headquarters.

"German Railroad Personnel!

In a fateful hour, the Führer has called us into action for the safety and peace of our Great German fatherland. I am certain that your always-ready courage and your ever-tested awareness of duty will also be proved in the coming days, and that you, whether at your usual workplace in the homeland or with a weapon in your hand, will give of yourselves to the last! In these historic hours, we greet our professional comrades in Danzig in heartiest unity, who after the return of Danzig to the Reich by the will of the Fuehrer, now have become again with outward right what you always have been inside: German railroad men!

German men of the flanged wheel! We all stand determined, in unbreakable loyalty, behind the Führer in the fight for the future of our splendid Reich!

Dorpmueller, Reich Traffic Minister and General Manager of the German Reichsbahn."
September 6, 1939.

In the autumn of 1939, the increased military traffic had to be handled, even after the Allied declaration of war. The British Navy began with a blockade that cut off the ocean traffic of all ships of the Axis Powers and limited the coastal traffic. Thus, a million tons of Ruhr coal per month for Italian industry, which until then had been shipped by sea, were now sent over the Alps by rail. A strict limitation of gasoline consumption for non-military purposes applied to the civilian traffic on the railroad.

After the Polish campaign, DRB administrations were established in Posen, Danzig, and Lodz. After a short time Lodz was shut down again, so that there were then 31 *Reichsbahn* administrative offices in all.

The strategically important double bridge over the Vistula at Tczev (Dirschau) was blown up by Polish forces in September 1939.

14

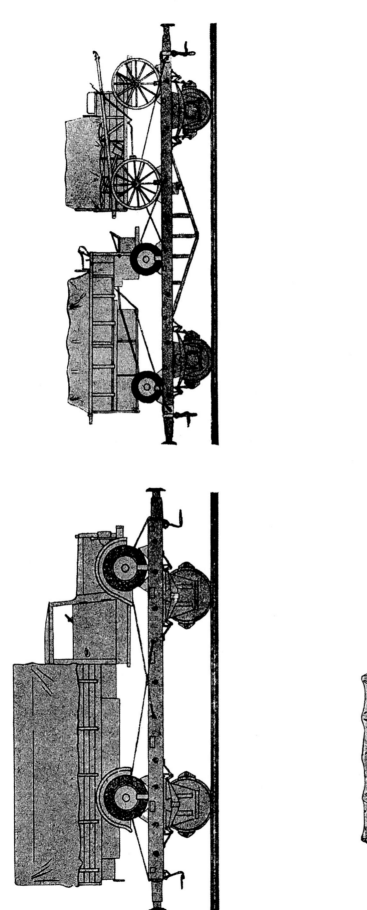
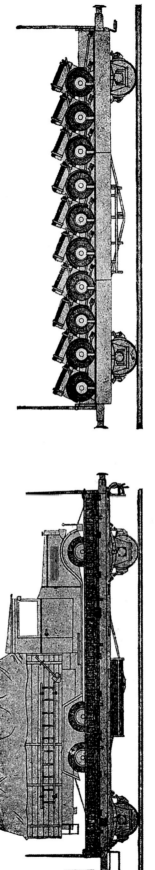

From: Army Service Regulations, 1940

Above: Winter 1939-40: a train moves laboriously along the Novy Targ-Krakau line.

Left: Winter 1939-40: this Polish Ty 23 locomotive got stuck in the snowdrifts shortly before reaching the Zakopane depot.

Krakau, Main Depot, autumn 1939: a police raid on Polish travelers.

Spring 1940, Warsaw Main Depot. While being built, it burned out in 1938. In September 1939 it took several direct hits, and by the rebellion in 1944 it was completely destroyed.

Berlin Anhalt Depot, autumn 1940: an express locomotive of 01⁰ Type 2C1-h1, Class S 36.20, built in 1935, with shaded lights.

Berlin Anhalt Depot, autumn 1940: a passenger locomotive (Prussian P 8), *Reichsbahn* series 38¹⁰, Type 2C-h2, Class P 35.17, built 1906-1922, with warning stripes on account of blackout use.

Autumn 1940: a blue railroad man on duty (inspector) wears the new uniform introduced in 1935.

2

Food Rationing Cards

"As of Monday, October 2, 1939, meals and foods can be dispensed in dining cars only in exchange for the appropriate sections of the cards distributed for the secure nourishment of the German people. The travelers must therefore carry their bread, meat, fat and grocery cards with them . . ."

German Information Bureau (DNB),
October 1, 1939

By the winter of 1939-40, almost the entire Polish railroad network was again open for traffic, and the German armies could be sent back from the Bug and San by rail. The large cities again received groceries and coal.

Hastening Car Turnaround

"To hasten the turnaround of railroad cars, the Reich Traffic Minister had arranged that Sundays and holidays on which, on account of the order of the Reich Economic Minister of November 30, 1939, railroad freight cars must be unloaded by the receiver, be regarded as working days

for the extent of the unloading time and the reckoning of the car money. For the cars not unloaded during this period, the specified car condition fee will be dropped on such Sundays and holidays."

DNB, December 1, 1939

Blackouts

"On the first trip during the blackout, it is very difficult, even for the locomotive engineer who knows the line, to find his way along the line and to the depots, since the completely dark surroundings show him a still-unfamiliar picture and make his orientation difficult. The locomotive engineer often recognizes the locations of signals, and especially landmarks, too late or not surely enough, which raises the danger of accidents. The Reich Traffic Minister has therefore, by order of November 23 of this year, instructed that the engineers who know the lines, which they have not yet driven during the blackout, are to make an instructional trip to refresh their memory under the difficult conditions. This measure is to be carried out as quickly as the personnel situation allows."

NSBZ Announcement, 12/17/1939

On January 15, 1940, decisive measures were made known for the entire Reich area. Along with a decrease in available extra-fare zones from five to three zones for express and other fast trains, a large part of the fare decreases that had traffic-attracting significance were dropped. In the future, for example, Sunday round-trip tickets, vacation tickets, [Zehner] and round-trip tickets were dropped. To unburden train personnel, on February 10, 1940, an added fare of 50 Pfennig for buying tickets on the train was introduced. After that, there were no essential fare changes to the end of the war.

German-Soviet Freight Shipping

"A direct German-Soviet freight fare is coming into being, which regulates traffic over nine border crossings, for which, as follows, the German and the Soviet border depots are lised: Szczepki/Augustow, Prostken/Grajevo, Malkin/Zaremba, Platerov, Siemiatytche, Terespol/Brest-Litovsk, Cholm/Yagodzin, Belzec-Rava Ruskaya, Zuravica/Peremyschl, Novy Zagorz/Salush. These crossings are opened immediately for freight traffic. For several days, whole trainloads of mineral oil and vegetables have been shipped. Only the opening of the Cholm/Yagodzin crossing is delayed somewhat, until the bridge over the Bug is rebuilt . . .

For the time being, the freight coming from the Soviet Union and destined for Germany will be reloaded into German freight cars at the border stations listed above. In the direction from Germany to the Soviet Union, the goods will be reloaded at the listed Soviet stations. Arrangements for passenger traffic will follow soon."

DNB, January 30, 1940

The railroad of the General government that consisted of part of occupied Poland is subordinated to a general directorship of the Ostbahn (Gedob) with its seat in Krakau. It belongs to the *Reichsbahn*, but remains the property of the General Government. The administration of the Gedob has a certain structure. The right to give instructions is thus divided between the Reich Traffic Minister and the General Governor. Included in the competence of the Reich Traffic Minister are: Traffic, activity, machine service, building, workshops, and administration of the German personnel. The General Governor, on the other hand, has the right to take part in decision-making in the realms of finance and fares, native personnel, social welfare, basic administration, and press. The structure of the Gedob was changed several times; the organization of the individual offices was finally determined in 1943.

Larger independent offices had a German principal and a small staff of German personnel. Other executive offices—especially on branch lines—were subordinate to depots and administrations with purely Polish personnel. In the improvement works, the overseeing personnel consisted of only two percent Germans; even masters and engineers were Poles or Ukrainians. For the troubled population of the General Government, the identity card of the *Ostbahn* soon became the most desirable form of identification, since it was still capable of protecting its holder from the arbitrary measures of the authorities and, at the same time, freeing them from the travel limitations for non-German persons.

In September 1940, Gedob President Gerteis informed General Governor Frank that the nourishment level of the Polish employees of the *Ostbahn* was catastrophic. The weakened stokers of the locomotives were no longer capable of shoveling coal into the boilers, for the Polish railroad men received only one-seventh as much food as a German worker in the Reich. The Polish workers generally worked willingly, although they were paid only two Pfennig per hour and often had to go hungry. Finally it was arranged by the Food Supply Office that the Polish railroad workers would also be given half a pound of bread and half a pound of meat, plus a few cigarettes during a trip. Because of the breakdowns of many engine personnel, though, the number of trains had to be reduced.

Home to the Reich on the Reichsbahn

On January 25, 1940, the hundred-thousandth of those resettled in the Reich crossed . . . the German-Russian boundary of interest . . . The railroad depots, some of them very small, with very primitive rail and loading facilities, that had been made into border stations by the creation of this boundary of interests, were from the start unable to handle the mass transit of resettlers,

and so they had to be expanded as fast as possible. The most unfavorable conditions were those in Przemysl, where there was no depot, for the Przemysl depot was on the Russian side. Some 80% of the resettlers were brought from the Russian side on trains and had to be loaded at the interest boundary, along with their extensive baggage, onto German trains, which were made up of 10 to 20 passenger cars; one of these trains held up to 1200 people.

The Russians brought the resettlement trains, partly on Russian broad gauge, partly on standard gauge, to the German side of the San bridge, and here the reloading had to be done on the track or at a junction. Only through extremely capable service of the railroad employees was it possible to carry out the set task and master the great difficulties."

DNB, April 27, 1940

Because of the hard frost in the first winter of the war, the ship traffic in Germany came to a full stop, which put even more of a burden on the shipment of freight. Snowdrifts, the steadily dwindling work force, overly long work hours, and increasing trouble with locomotives greatly influenced the DRB's capability. As the war went on, business traffic also increased, particularly in the most important industrial centers. The "hamster" trips to the country, visits of wounded men and *Wehrmacht* furlough traffic all increased. General Gercke reserved numerous spare locomotives and cars for various operations, which also increased the lack of rolling stock. Disagreements between Gercke and higher *Reichsbahn* officials, the Coal Commissioner, and industry were daily events.

Main Railroad Car Office

"In order to bring the movement of empty cars into connection with carrying out business, the Main Car Office, as of April 1, 1940, is subordinated to the General Business Command East. The Main Car Office, with the offices that belong to it, forms an independent department, including the former Department III of the Reichsbahn Central Office in Berlin, with the same composition as previously. In the direct cooperation of the Main Car Office with the Reichsbahn management, namely in supplying the operations in the individual Reichsbahn management offices with cars, nothing has changed . . ."

DNB, February 25, 1940

An easing in the management of supplying was brought about by the institution of the "train divider," who determined the debt payments on individual lines by trains heading toward the front. At the beginning of 1941, administrative offices took over the direction of supplies. First came the Direction Office East in Warsaw; later the Direction Office Southeast in Vienna was established. They had the task of assuring that all supplying matched the needs of the troops and the capacities of the DRB. Only thanks to the activity of the direction offices and train dividers did supply trains run more smoothly.

Permission Tickets

"The *Reichsbahn*, because it is heavily burdened with military tasks and the freight traffic necessary for survival, cannot sufficiently handle increased passenger traffic at Pentecost and thus asks repeatedly that unnecessary travel on the coming holidays not be done. In order to maintain order in long-range traffic, in the period from Thursday, May 9, 6:00 P.M. to Tuesday, May 14, 12:00 midnight (except Pentecost Sunday), specified express and fast trains that will be listed by the Reichsbahn management . . . may be used only with special permission tickets. Excused from the obtaining of permission tickets are travelers crossing the border, travelers with Wehrmacht tickets, possessors of time, network and district tickets, and tickets for berths in sleeping cars.

The permission tickets are to be obtained along with travel tickets and will be issued free of charge in chronological order and in limited numbers, as long as the supplies for the individual trains suffice, by the ticket dispensers and travel bureaus indicated by the Reichsbahn management . . .

The permission tickets guarantee neither a right to travel nor a seat or a place in the car class of the ticket. The validity of the ticket begins only on the day for which the permission ticket was obtained. The latter is to be returned after the end of the trip, along with the used travel ticket. Travelers who want to make a return trip during the banned time with a limited-availability train from one of the named cities must there obtain a special permission ticket for the return trip. If they can no longer obtain one for the desired train, then they will have to wait for another time to return; so that they prepare themselves for this contingency in advance, they are hereby reminded very particularly.

Whoever uses a train unjustly without a permission ticket is liable to be excluded from the trip and to be punished by the railroad police . . ."

DNB, May 3, 1940

The advance in the winter and spring of 1940 before the western campaign against France, Belgium, Holland, and Luxembourg involved 136 divisions. Because of the heavy motorizing of the Army, there were scarcely any difficulties in supplying, even in the western campaign. The railroad could follow the fast-moving operation only slowly because of the widespread destruction of the traffic routes, and therefore contributed little to the results.

The railroad engineers rebuilt the main lines of the French State Railroad (SNCF) in record time. Dr. Dorpmueller, the German Traffic Minister and also the General Manager of the *Reichsbahn*, could already ride a train to Paris on July 18, 1940, three weeks after the surrender, and expressed his recognition of the gray railroad men of the *Wehrmacht* for this achievement.

During the armistice, the French railroad system was divided into two zones. The lines in unoccupied France fell under the control of the Vichy Government, while those of the occupied area were directed by a civilian administration in Paris, under German oversight. The railroads of Alsace and Lorraine were turned over to the German *Reichsbahn*.

In occupied France and Belgium, *Wehrmacht* traffic administrations (WVD) were at first set up, with headquarters in Paris and Brussels, subordinate to the Chief of Transportation. One authority each was ordered to Lyon and Toulouse in unoccupied France. The leadership, though, remained with the SNCF.

In August 1940 the *Wehrmacht* traffic administration in Paris came fully into action under the military command of Colonel Goeritz. The position of the railroad workers in this semi-military position was imaginably bad. They had as good as no independence, but were there only to carry out *Wehrmacht* orders.

To supervise the railroad activity, there were—because of a constantly feared general strike by the French railroad personnel—some 35,000 blue railroad men ready in France, Belgium, and Holland. But they never—against expectation—needed to intervene at full strength, but served mainly to carry out oversight tasks.

The German military planned to place the French electric locomotives in their war service, but were never in a situation to adapt these electric motors from 1500-volt direct current to the necessary one-phase alternating current.

The actions of the French Resistance, an underground movement directed by followers of General de Gaulle, who operated from London, caused many new problems for the German military.

In November 1940, a freight train with French war prisoners was attacked by the Resistance, and several hundred soldiers were able to flee. In July 1941 the French railroad workers merged with the secret "Combat" organization. As of 1942 the Germans deported several thousand French railroad workers. They were sent to do forced labor in Germany, and settled at the larger railroad junctions east of the Rhine, where they were exposed to the heaviest Allied air raids. More than 20,000 of these people would never see their homeland again. For the French railroads too, there soon began a long period of systematic serious destruction by Allied bombing. But it had not become that bad yet.

Reshipment Place for Those on Furlough

"The German word 'Urlaub' has a very special sound for soldiers, which can be judged correctly only by a soldier who has been on furlough. But scarcely any of those lucky ones who receive furlough papers and train tickets from the orderly room think about what kind of significant demands the furlough traffic makes on the offices of the Wehrmacht or the railroad, and what a big, inclusive organization has to be on hand to assure the smooth operation of furlough traffic amid the ever-growing pressure on the Reichsbahn. To be able to look behind the facade of this organization, we visited one of the focal points of furlough traffic, a depot from which numerous SF (fast furlough) trains are sent out every day to all parts of Germany. There we came into the middle of the great pack of furloughed men, many of whom pass through this station en route to their homes every day. Several SF trains had arrived from the west, and a mass of field gray, sea blue and gray-blue uniforms swirled together, also including members of the Organisation Todt, the Technical Emergency Help and some civilians. All the happy faces and laughter said: Now we're going on furlough! With cheering, encouraging words, the new arrivals were directed by a voice on the loudspeaker into one of two large gathering places across from the depot. Here the furloughed men were grouped for transport to the individual German depots and divided among the individual SF trains.

From early morning to late afternoon, there was much happening in the place. At the information booth the soldiers were advised of the best travel routes. At the change booth they could change their money to German currency. Naturally, there was a big crowd at the post office; several hundred telegrams and telephone calls go out from here daily to relatives and advise them "mercifully" of the news. Whoever is on furlough naturally wants to bring his loved ones something. So the men heading for home usually arrive at the scene heavily burdened with parcels. Part of their parcels can be sent by mail, and the numbers of the parcels and small packets sent from there reach almost astronomical totals. Whoever wants to leave the site during his stay, which often last for several hours, can leave his luggage at the official baggage room.

Feeding the furloughed men is taken care of in a model procedure. At several mobile kitchens, great quantities can be cooked for the always-hungry crowds of soldiers and served in nicely appointed waiting rooms by

Red Cross nurses. Thus the furloughed men spend their time in the best of moods, conversing, reading, playing cards and hearing music from the loudspeaker, until the microphone calls them: 'Furloughed men in Direction E . . .step forward!'

The furlough traffic that must pass through these junctions is so heavy that traffic from Germany to the front cannot be handled at the same depots; it uses the freight stations a few kilometers away. There we find the same scenes: With happy faces, after having enjoyed pleasant furloughs, the men arriving from Germany wait to be sent on to the front, treated splendidly here as well during their

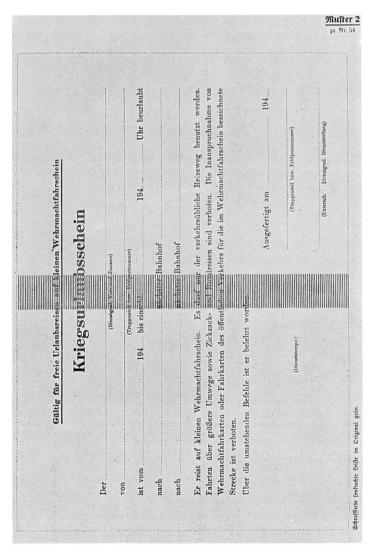

One of the furlough forms for members of the German *Wehrmacht*.

Die Russenlieferungen rollen

Auf Grund der verschiedenen Abmachungen mit Sowjetrussland findet ein lebhafter Warenaustausch zwischen dem Grossdeutschen Reiche und Russland statt. Diese Tatsache erweckt bei vielen Menschen das Interesse, wie denn dieser Warenaustausch vor sich geht.

Vor allem steht die Eisenbahn in seinem Dienste. Zur Regelung dieses Güterverkehrs ist, wie wir der Reichsbahn-Beamten-Zeitung entnehmen, bereits am 29. Dezember 1939 zwischen dem Reichsverkehrsministerium und dem Volkskommissariat für Verkehrswesen der UdSSR. ein vorläufiges Eisenbahngrenzabkommen geschlossen worden, das am 1. Oktober 1940 durch ein endgültiges deutsch-sowjetisches Grenzabkommen für den Personen-, Gepäck-, Expressgut- und Güterverkehr ersetzt worden ist. Für die Grenzübergangsbahnhöfe und die Strecken zwischen ihnen sind besondere Bahnanlagen geschaffen worden. Personen, Gepäck, Expressgut und andere Güter in der Richtung aus dem Deutschen Reich nach UdSSR. werden mit den deutschen Wagen bis in den sowjetischen Grenzübergangsbahnhof, und in der Richtung aus der UdSSR. nach dem Deutschen Reich mit den sowjetischen Wagen bis in den deutschen Grenzübergangsbahnhof befördert. Da die deutschen Eisenbahnen eine Spurweite von 1435 Millimetern und die sowjetischen Eisenbahnen, soweit sie umgespurt sind, eine solche von 1524 Millimetern haben, sind die Grenzübergangsbahnhöfe und die Strecken zwischen ihnen so eingerichtet, dass die Züge der Eisenbahnen jeder Seite bis zum Grenzübergangsbahnhof der anderen Seite fahren können. Zu diesem Zweck sind zwischen den Grenzübergangsbahnhöfen zwei besondere Streckengeleise erforderlich ein Gleis mit Normalspur und ein Gleis der Breitspur. Diese Geleise liegen entweder nebeneinander oder ineinander. Ueber den Grenzübergangsbahnhof der fremden Bahn hinaus dürfen keine Wagen fahren, auch nicht die für den Radsatzwechsel besonders gebauten Umsetzwagen. Die Personen müssen umsteigen; die Gepäck-, Expressgut- und Gütersendungen werden in Wagen der Empfangsbahn umgeladen. Für die Uebergabezüge zwischen den Grenzübergangsbahnhöfen werden Regel- und Bedarfsfahrpläne vereinbart, die der grösstmöglichen Dauerleistung der beiden Bahnhöfe entsprechen. Das Zugmeldeverfahren ist ziemlich schwerfällig und umständlich. Wenn man den Vorschriften beider Seiten gerecht werden wollte, gab es keine andere Lösung. Die Züge werden telegraphisch angeboten, angenommen, abgemeldet und zurückgemeldet. Der Wortlaut der Zugmeldung ist genau festgelegt. Die Meldungen werden in das Zugmeldebuch eingetragen. Sie werden deutscherseits in deutscher Sprache und sowjetischerseits in russischer Sprache gegeben.

Wenn die telegraphische Verbindung unterbrochen ist, werden die Zugmeldungen auf dem Fernsprecher gegeben. Ist auch der Fernsprecher gestört, so wird durch Vermittlung von Boten eine schriftliche Verständigung darüber herbeigeführt, wie der Zugverkehr aufrechterhalten werden soll. Mit der deutsch-sowjetischen Grenze fällt die Zeitgrenze zwischen mitteleuropäischer und Moskauer Zeit zusammen. Im Uebergangsverkehr wenden die Bediensteten die Zeit an, die in dem Gebiet gültig ist, in dem sie sich aufhalten. Bekanntlich hat die Moskauer Zeit gegenüber der mitteleuropäischen Zeit zwei Stunden und gegenüber der deutschen Sommerzeit eine Stunde Vorsprung. Die Uebergabezüge nach der UdSSR. werden durch das Lokomotiv- und Zugpersonal der deutschen Eisenbahn bis in die sowjetische Grenzübergangshöfe, die Uebergabezüge nach dem Deutschen Reich durch die Lokomotiven und das Zugpersonal der sowjetischen Eisenbahn bis in die deutschen Grenzübergangsbahnhöfe gefahren. Leere Wagen werden durch Lokomotiven und Personal der Eigentumsverwaltung zurückgefahren. Die Signale auf den Grenzübergangsbahnhöfen und auf den Strecken zwischen ihnen werden durch die Vorschriften der Seite bestimmt, auf deren Gebiet sie stehen. Das Personal, das die Uebergabezüge während der Fahrt auf dem Gebiet der anderen Seite bedient, muss daher die Betriebs- und Signalvorschriften dieser Seite kennen. Auf Forderung der sowjetischen Bahnen dürfen die Züge nur mit der Lokomotive an der Spitze fahren. Das Rangieren hat jeder Bahnhof mit den eigenen Lokomotiven und dem eigenen Personal durchzuführen. Bei Unterbrechungen oder Störungen des normalen Zugverkehrs benachrichtigen sich die beiden Bahnhöfe telegraphisch und leisten sich gegenseitig Beistand. Jede Seite sorgt in ihrem Bereich für die Bewachung der Uebergabezüge durch das Zugpersonal. Die Bediensteten der einen Seite wenden auch auf dem Gebiete der anderen Seite die eigene Sprache an. Beide Seiten müssen wegen der gegenseitigen Verständigung auf den Grenzübergangsbahnhöfen mindestens einen Bediensteten haben, der die Sprache der anderen Seite beherrscht. Schriftliche Befehle für das Zugpersonnal werden in den beiden amtlichen Sprachen ausgefertigt. Für den übrigen Dienstverkehr bedient sich jede Seite der eigenen Amtssprache.

Das Deutsch-Sowjetische Eisenbahn-Grenzabkommen in seiner Form und in dem Geist seiner Anwendung ist ein besonderer Erfolg für die gegenseitige Verbindung und für den gegenseitigen Warenaustausch beider Völker, der sich in seiner wirklichen Grösse erst nach der Neuordnung Europas und der Welt richtig erkennen lassen wird.

From the Berliner Boersen-Zeitung (Stock Market Newspaper), January 1941.

Spring 1940, Euskirchen near Bonn: in the background is a DB locomotive of the 38^{10} series.

At a Paris depot in the summer of 1940: the French railroad man with his new bosses.

A makeshift bridge built near Reims in the summer of 1940 is tested for load capacity by a freight locomotive of the former French Northern Railway.

France, summer 1940: a makeshift bridge over the Loire with a French passenger locomotive, No. 141,050 of the Western Region.

Winter 1940: a railroad bridge over the Vienne in France.

On the German lines somewhere between Cologne and the west, 1940: an autumn day begins.

Calais, September 1940: a 28-cm medium railroad gun on two five-axle turntable cars.

November 1940: a DR placard.

The running sign of a special furlough train (SF) in 1940.

The train reaches the Parisian suburb of St. Cloud. It is April 15, 1941, 8:00 AM, and the men are going to work.

Norway, May 1941, at the ore harbor, Narvik: on a three-rail line for broad and standard gauge are two freight cars with brakemen's huts.

Gare St. Lazare, Paris, 1941.

A railroad crossing near Reims, late May 1941: two former enemies, a French and a German railroad man, work side by side.

3

When Hitler gave the order on July 21, 1940, to prepare for war against the Soviet Union, the *Wehrmacht* insisted on extending the eastern railroad lines. The so-called "Otto Program" called for extending rail lines from west to east and creating better loading capacities at the Soviet border.

In December 1940, the Army High Command instructed that the advance would take eight weeks, and could no longer be concealed from mid-April 1941 on. The hitherto peaceful development of eastern lines was finally ended. On February 4, 1941, a conference was held at the headquarters of the *Ostbahn* administration in Krakow, and all the administrators of the railroad and the military transport system took part. The purpose of this meeting was to attain full utilization of the *Ostbahn* railroad capacities.

The advance on the USSR created the greatest tasks known by the railroads to date.

The first months of 1941 were marked by preparations for the eastern campaign.

Iron Rations

"Through several distributions of mixed foods, the Reichsbahn management is in a position to satisfy the provision needs of locomotive and train crews, caused by delays in train arrivals, by distributing mixed foods as iron rations. Carrying out these measures must be assured above all in the cases in which the crew members know from experience that they will have no time or chance to eat at a business or works kitchen or a depot canteen."

DNB, January 11, 1941

Under strictest secrecy, the greatest railroad advance in history began. Even through the whole of troop preparation, the exchange of freight with the Soviet Union continued smoothly. For Operation "Barbarossa," the attack on the Soviet Union, and its preparations, a total of 33,800 trains were in use, a unique achievement of the German *Reichsbahn*. The network of the *Ostbahn* was never once used in its full extent thereby.

"The foreign press has published several reports in the last few weeks, saying that the rail traffic between Germany and the Soviet Union, regulated by the Moscow Accords of December 1939, and particularly the traffic between Romania and Germany over the Soviet Oraseni-Peremysl (Przemysl) line, was not to function . . . All of these reports are fully inaccurate. The through traffic between Germany and Romania through the Soviet Union is moving without problems, many hundreds of cars have already passed over the Soviet through line. The shipping of grain and mineral oils from Russia is also in full operation, and several thousand cars have been moved already."

DNB, May 15, 1941

More than in any other theater of war, the fortunes of war on the eastern front depended on functioning railroads. During the first weeks of the campaign, the *Wehrmacht* learned that modern armies could not be supplied sufficiently on the simple Russian road network, especially during the autumnal rainy season, when the roads turned into a single swamp. Thus, the most important military goal for both sides was to get control of the sometimes well-built rail network. For this reason, the German High command insisted that Hitler give Army Group Center priority in the advance on Moscow, so as to take over the main junction point there. With success near, Hitler was indecisive and did not listen to his generals' advice.

The White Coat

"The Reich Traffic Minister has significantly extended and changed the service clothing orders for the German Reichsbahn. Along with the service uniform, a service uniform for special occasions is also introduced . . . For the warmer season in hot regions, the introduction of a very light coat with an open collar has proved to be necessary. Here only a white coat of either linen or cotton cloth can be considered. The delivery of this piece of clothing depends on the possibility of timely and sufficient provision of this cloth. With it, only white clothing with a black tie may be worn. That this piece of clothing should be worn in a strictly clean condition must be regarded as self-evident. Otherwise it is better not to wear the white coat. As for trousers, only long trousers with red piping can be considered."

NSBZ-Voraus, August 1941

Although most of the bridges had been destroyed by the *Luftwaffe* and by Soviet troops during their retreat, the German railroad engineers were almost always able to keep the lines to the front usable.

The decisive problem was the broad gauge of 1524 mm on the Russian railroads. For the Germans, this meant constant reloading of freight or revision of the tracks, along with dozens of other technical difficulties. In the other occupied countries, the problem was even worse: Estonia used broad gauge, Latvia broad and standard gauge, and Lithuania standard gauge. The building of the broad-gauge Russian railways in the 19th century was based on the strategic consideration of making the use of the lines by foreign vehicles difficult.

The increasing shortage of broad-gauge locomotives and cars urgently compelled the revising of the Russian broad-gauge tracks to standard gauge. One rail was moved 9 cm inward, and in this way the track could be used on the main advance routes. More quickly than it was thought to be possible, the revision took place; the broad-gauge material must be moved to the front soon, for standard gauge is already in use from the rear. The work columns respike ten kilometers of rails and more in one day. In fact, 15,000 kilometers of track were respiked by the end of 1941, but east of the Dniepr the broad-gauge traffic still dominated for a long time.

Respiked! Soviet Lines with German Gauge

"In his speech of October 3, 1941, the Fuehrer and Supreme Commander related that in the captured area in the East, 15,000 kilometers of Soviet railroads have already been respiked by our railroad engineers. Meanwhile, these tracks will have been lengthened considerably, so that a major part of the Soviet railroad network has been made usable for supplying with German locomotives.

As is known, the gauge of the railroad lines in Germany, as in most countries of the world, measures 1435 millimeters. The Soviet tracks, on the other hand, have a gauge of 1524 millimeters, thus some ten centimeters wider than the German standard gauge.

It is technically not possible to equalize the track gauge with the German by laying a new rail beside the present one. The simplest and, above all, cheapest method is respiking, which means moving one rail nine centimeters inward. This sounds considerably simpler than it really is. The great achievements that must be carried out can only be attained by extraordinary cooperation of the individual facilities. It consists of the following main processes: Loosening the rail spikes, evening the ties at the new positions, and moving and attaching the rails. Beyond that, on curves, because of the 9-centimeter shorter radius of the one rail, the curve of the rail also changes. On curves with a very large radius, the difference, to be sure, is scarcely important. Along with that, under circumstances, the elevation of the outer rail must also be changed.

Certain difficult situations also arise in switches because of the crossing of the rails, so that new pieces of rail must usually be installed. There is also the care that must be given to the roadbed, since the center of gravity of the rolling stock is displaced somewhat by the shortening of the track gauge. On curves and double-rack roadbeds, the outer rail must therefore always be moved inward, so that the pressure of the train moves inward more than outward.

From these small bits of information it will be seen what tremendous achievements our railroad engineers are accomplishing in the East, quite apart from the rebuilding of railroad bridges. The significance of these achievements for our supplying may also be seen in the fact that by far the greater part of the double-track rail lines in the Soviet Union is in German hands."

Die Wehrmacht, 1941

Among the enormous increase in *Reichsbahn* performance, the troop movements and supplying play a dominant role. From February 15 to June 19, 1941, a total of 11,784 trains with some 200,000 cars covered an average distance of 800 km for the advance against the USSR. Astonishingly, these movements were carried out successfully along with the normal schedules. Only on May 22, 1941, a month before the attack on the Soviet Union, was the so-called highest-performance schedule introduced, with a maximum capacity of nearly 3000 trains per day.

Special Furlough
"Female followers of the German *Reichsbahn*, whose husbands were away from home for at least three months by being called to military service, are on their request concerning the presence of their husbands on furlough from the *Wehrmacht*, to be released from service on twelve days of the year. The wife's recreational vacation is to be reckoned on this time; for the excess part, release from service is to be guaranteed without further payment of salary or bonuses."

DNB, September 1, 1941

It came as a complete surprise that there were troop movements for a campaign against Yugoslavia to be commenced shortly. This difficult railroad-military task was carried out on schedule. The simultaneous advance on the Soviet Union had to be carried out mainly on six transport lines, and went off almost problem-free after initial difficulties.

The Balkan campaign meant further supply problems, for whole areas of land were only slightly touched by transit and scarcely passable. The operations in the mountainous country required transit structures that went far beyond the normal extent. Only in May 1941 did the Field Railroad Administration (FBD), headquartered in Belgrade, begin its work. The operations could very soon be turned over to the Greek and Yugoslavian railroads. Greece, Bulgaria, Romania, Hungary, and Slovakia carried on their railroad activities somewhat independently throughout the war.

The close cooperation with Romania and the extensive investments that the DRB made for transit lines there had favorable effects on the eastern campaign. When a crisis on the eastern front in 1943 threatened Army Group South, the security of Transnistria [?] and Bessarabia was of great importance as a supply base. Therefore Hitler suggested to Antonescu that the railroad operations be put in German hands. But the dictator turned this down energetically.

To secure the transport routes, a "Special Authority for the Maintenance of Danube Ship Traffic" was set up on June 20, 1944, by means of which coordinated measures for a temporary improvement of transport conditions were instituted. The rebuilding of the railroad lines succeeded, and crude oil transport reached 70% of its normal level at that time. The change of the front in Romania hit German gasoline supplying and shipping to the Balkans all the harder.

In the course of the war from 1941 to 1945, Yugoslavian partisans destroyed 1684 km of railroad tracks, 830 depots, 1099 trains, 1918 locomotives, 19,759 cars, and 1077 railroad bridges.

A Christmas Tree for Everyone

"For the third time, the German people are preparing for a war Christmas. Even though many nice things are not available as they were in peacetime, everyone would like to be able to decorate his Christmas tree. But often the fir trees must travel a long way on the train before they get from the forests to the Christmas-tree markets. Therefore the German *Reichsbahn* has, despite the great demands on its freight cars, given directions this year as in the past that the freight cars needed for the transport of Christmas trees, whenever possible, be provided fully. Even though here and there the requested cars may have to be waited for, everyone can count on the *Reichsbahn* delivering his Christmas tree."

DNB, November 25, 1941

The Reich Traffic Minister announced on March 13, 1942:

Use of Sleeping Cars by Married Couples

"In the present traffic situation it cannot be permitted that two first-class bed spaces be reserved for married couples. I have therefore given instructions that two first-class bed tickets must not be given to married couples."

Army Instruction Sheet, April 8, 1942

March 1941: Biala-Podlaska, a small but important station on the Berlin-Warsaw-Brest Litovsk-Smolensk-Moscow line. The calm before the storm …

Spring 1941: on the important Krakow-Przemysl line, Polish youths forcibly recruited for "building service" are laying new rails

On the line between Krakow and Przemysl, March 1941: the advance on the Soviet Union.

This shock troop poses for the cameraman at a Russian station in July 1941. At right is a locomotive of the "Josef Stalin" JS-20 series, at left a captured machine gun.

Tarnolop, summer 1941: the railroad bridge was blown up by the Russians.

Lower left: a rail-truck at Luzk, summer 1941.

Right: the end of an information trip, summer 1941: The enemy took the rail away.

Valuable, rare booty: several Russian condenser locomotives of the SO-19 series between Polonnoye and Berdishev, July 15, 1941.

A safe hiding place by a sidetrack near Stalingrad-South, September 1942.

Ten thousand kilometers of respiked rails are checked by the Main Railroad Direction South (Kiev). The four-axle freight car of 1917 houses the railroad engineers.

Autumn 1941, Terespol, a station not far from Brest-Litovsk: a Russian tank car at the wheel-switching site.

A Russian factory locomotive up on the lifting tackle, ready for wheel-changing.

Left, top down:
Changing wheels is hard work.

A turntable in the wheel-changing works.

Railroad engineers work on a wheel profile.

Wehrmacht personnel car, rebuilt from a DR excursion car, France 1941.

Rethel, autumn 1941: a spooky passenger.

Autumn 1941: everyday work at the Brest-Litovsk freight station.

A former DR baggage car,
rebuilt as a kitchen car.
Eastern front, 1941.

A shoemaker's and tailor's shop in a former baggage car. Lemberg 1941.

A writing room in a baggage car. Lemberg 1941.

4

The conquered Eastern Galicia with its capital of Lemberg was joined to the General Government. From the railroad men assigned to the General Government, the Main Railroad Administration South (HBD Sued) was made up. The blue railroad personnel formed four main railroad administration offices, later established in Riga, Minsk, Kiev, and Dniepropetrovsk. As a command position for the blue railroad men, the German military founded the "Operations Administration East at the Chief of Transport" (BLO) in Warsaw. From this was developed on January 14, 1942, the "Branch Office East of the Reich Traffic Ministry" (Osteis), and on December 1, 1942, the "General Traffic Direction East" (GVD Osten). From then on, this GVD supervised all railroad activity in the occupied part of the Soviet Union. At the same time, a directive from Minister Dorpmueller changed the Main Railroad Directions into Reich Traffic Directions (RVD). The lines between the eastern boundaries of these offices and the front were subordinate to the Field Railroad Commands (FEKdo) 4, 2, 3, and 5, but the border areas between RVD and FEKdo changed constantly according to the position of the front. The Bialystok district had a special status:

it belonged neither to the *Ostbahn* nor the RVD Osten. With the long distances in the Soviet Union, the dearth of roads and the wide mesh of the rail network, the few railroad lines constantly gained in value. Despite all the hindrance by partisans, service could be maintained, even in the hardest-hit district of Minsk. Thus, the General Traffic Administration East reported that in April 1943 the transport of 1.67 million tons of freight had been possible. That corresponds to the highest achievement of October 1942. The railroad offices responsible for the general operation of the DRB were more or less helpless in the face of their tasks, since they were not yet equipped for action right behind the front lines. The field-gray railroad men under the command of the *Wehrmacht* took along everything on their advance that they could find: pumps, telephones, tools, lanterns, even railcars. Supplying the blue railroad men with food and other goods was also badly organized at first. Only in time could the actions of the military offices to guarantee cars only for themselves be stopped. On October 3, 1941, the Traffic Ministry ordered that lettering captured railroad cars "Deutsche Wehrmacht" by the military was to cease.

The "Blues" were in a particularly difficult position in their activities. Despite their meager military training, they were called on to defend the railway lines in addition to doing their regular tasks. They had no steel helmets, marching equipment, or assault kits. The "Blues," when in enemy country, did not enjoy the protection of the Geneva Convention as opposed to the soldiers, but were outside the law of war. The Russians killed the "Blues" as they did armed soldiers when they got their hands on them.

For mutual understanding between German and Russian workers for the DRB, multilingual illustrated booklets were often used, since interpreters were not on hand.

The German railroad men with the *Ostbahn* and the German *Reichsbahn* were regarded as heavy workers. They were issued at least 2000 grams of bread, 200 grams of meat (when moving, 100 grams more), 150 grams of fat (50 grams more when moving), and 5 kilograms of potatoes (7 kilo more when moving).

To differentiate their functions, the German railroad men wore colored armbands, while the local men wore blue bands with "Deutsche Reichsbahn" lettering. In the construction platoons, foreigners had gray armbands with "on task for the German Reichsbahn" lettering. The German, foreign and local employees of the building firms wore yellow armbands with "in the name of the German Reichsbahn" lettering. The position of the Administrator of the *Reichsbahn* (BvRb) between military transport command posts and organs of the gray and blue railroad units was a makeshift solution caused by the false organization of the *Wehrmacht* transport system. In addition, the effectiveness of this arrangement depended too strongly on the personality of the administrator at any time. Some of them, for lack of experience, were not in a position to prevail against the *Wehrmacht* service offices.

The trimmed announcements about the accomplishments of the lines in the winter of 1941-42 led to a new determination of the competence in the building, maintenance, and operation of the railroads in the occupied part of the Soviet Union. As ordered on January 4, 1942, the blue railroaders were again subordinated to the Traffic Minister and no longer to the *Wehrmacht*.

The situation in occupied Belgium and France got worse rapidly early in 1943. Many requisitions for locomotives lowered the numbers of vehicles increasingly. Besides, air raids limited activity, and the local personnel could no longer be depended on. In 1943 an extended campaign of railroad sabotage by active members of the resistance movement was begun. With the full support of the local railroaders, they derailed military trains, blew up tunnels, bridges, and many German security facilities, and cut telephone and telegraph lines.

Since the autumn of 1943, these destructive acts increased particularly on the lines in the Ardennes, around Liege in Belgium, around Lille and Paris, and on the Swiss border. With little air defense, the low-flying Allied planes especially liked to attack locomotives in the coastal areas, since they had a free and favorable field of operations there. In the district of the "Transport Command of Lille" alone, some 30 to 40 locomotives were destroyed, and in the West as a whole, three or four were lost every day. Supply and construction transports for the U-boats and the Atlantic Wall were badly disturbed. To hasten repairs, 18,000 men of the Organisation Todt had to be called away from the Atlantic Wall, which again had an unfavorable effect on its further construction.

In France itself, chaotic transport conditions grew by the day. In October 1943 the coal supply was enough for only six weeks, decreasing to four in November and in December to two.

Considerable Improvement

"The good progress in the rebuilding of destroyed tracks, in which German railroad engineers and German companies were involved through action at important building sites, made the carrying out of considerable improvements in the coming summer schedule by improving transit speeds and choosing more favorable routes for both Wehrmacht furlough traffic and public transport.

For example, the present travel time of an SF train from Biarritz to Homburg (Saar), compared to the time taken by this train at its inception in July 1940, is now 18 hours shorter. The business and service traffic that has grown more and more in recent times could be handled by adding new trains and improving train connections."

DNB, October-November 1942

At the beginning of 1943, medium and heavy bombers as well as fighter-bombers of the 8th and 9th U.S. Air Fleets flew thousands of missions against French and Belgian railroad facilities for two months, with the goal of destroying them totally. By D-Day, the air raids had knocked three quarters of the two thousand locomotives in northern France out of service.

The French Resistance accomplished 600 train derailments, and destroyed 1800 locomotives and 6000 cars just from January to June 1944 in the course of its "Plan Vert," which called for the total destruction of German supply lines on the eve of the Allied landing.

The anti-railroad war of the Maquis resulted especially in the German troops sent to Normandy from France or neighboring fronts being either delayed or arriving in a decimated condition. Three armored divisions that were sent on the march by the German High Command reached the theater of war only with much delay and by roundabout routes. The 17th Armored Division, which was to be ready for action in two days, lost some ten days to Resistance action between Bordeaux and Poitiers.

The 2nd SS Armored Division "Das Reich" left Montauban headed for Normandy on 6 June, but since all the railroad lines were at a standstill and their units were held up by Maqui attacks in the Departments of Tarn, Lot, Correze, and Haute-Vienne, they reached their destination—beaten—only on 18 June. The transfer of the 11th Armored Division from the eastern front to France took 31 days. To be sure, they reached the French border in eight days, but needed 23 days to get from Strasbourg to Caen.

The lack of supplies at the time of the Normandy landing also contributed to the onset of German losses. Regulated rail traffic was already impossible in France as of May 1944, and vehicles and fuel for road transport were lacking. And before June 6, 1944, the Seine bridges downstream from Paris and all the Loire bridges below Orleans were destroyed. Thus, the Germans set up a very well-organized and extensive ferry service, which was, of course, bombed for days by the Allies during the German retreat.

Reichsbahn and Invasion

"At the beginning of the invasion, the German Reichsbahn, which had until then overseen and directed the work of the French railroads at supervision offices, administrative offices and command positions with comparatively meager powers, was now given a particularly responsible task. For years the work of the German railroad men in the West had been almost like peacetime, only slightly disturbed by air raids or attacks such as the railroaders in the East experienced daily. That had now changed. The invasion had alerted the railroaders by the weeks of bombings of transit routes, operating facilities and depots, and now that the battle raged on the invasion front, the slogan of the German railroaders in Germany, "We're moving anyway!" and that of the railroaders in the East, "Go, go, just keep going!" were supposed to be turned into deeds in the West as well.

We drove in a car through the lovely green landscape of Normandy. For kilometers, the backlands lay in deepest peace. One could forget the war, if only ruins along the roads—even of DRK trucks and civilian vehicles—would warn us to beware of low-flying enemy planes.

Up to the front lines we met only the blue uniforms of the German railroaders. We found the same spirit that made their tremendous accomplishments in the East possible, that inspired the men of Kovel. Despite the heaviest bombing raids that tore up the tracks, sank locomotives and cars in bomb craters, despite gunfire from the low-flying planes, the wheels rolled. The French railroad man also handled his tasks with commendable loyalty.

With tremendous effort, enemy bomber groups have bombed the railroad facilities. Every time we came near a large freight station, bomb mats that had failed in their mission and torn-up fields and meadows told us that it was near. A bridge that a few German dive bombers had destroyed in a 1940 raid was struck only after repeated attacks by strong enemy groups.

But even though the destruction seemed so severe at first glance, German and French railroad men got to work at once, filled the bomb craters, operated the cranes that moved the ruins out of the way. Engineers worked hard to build makeshift bridges over the rivers in a remarkably short time. By the work columns stood sentries, who gave the alarm when enemy fighters came near. At the building sites—as on all the roads, short distances apart—anti-splinter ditches had been dug.

As the Anglo-American fighter pilots fired their weapons ruthlessly, even at women and children, they also attacked transport and passenger trains and locomotives. Many German and French locomotive drivers have had to give their lives in loyal fulfillment of their duty to the last. But again and again their comrades climb into the locomotives. An astonishing example of awareness of duty and proof that a great number of the French have understood the meaning of our life-and-death struggle was given by an old French locomotive driver. Two of his sons had fallen victim to the foreign fighter planes, and yet he went on driving his trains as before.

Meanwhile, especially on the lines nearest the front and thus most damaged, German personnel have taken over the work, in order to assure supplying the front despite the most difficult conditions.

At a small depot, heavy tanks were being unloaded. The transport trains had to be unloaded as quickly as possible, so that the enemy air reconnaissance could not see that the tank formations would be going into action. The German switchman, who wore in his buttonhole the ribbons of the War Service Cross and the East Medal, was experienced in switching the special cars that carried the tanks and unloading transport trains. There is probably no better recognition of their work, which is also recognition for all railroaders, than the words that the unit leader of the tank formation spoke to us: "I don't need to worry about the unloading; the Blues always do that. And faster than they do it, that's simply impossible!"—Over the ramp erected of beams and rails the previous day, the heavy tanks and vehicles now roll. The tracks of the heavy treads are carefully obliterated, vehicles and equipment are hidden under trees and shrubs. At night they then begin their march to the front.

We are astonished to see the fortifications of the Atlantic Wall. How many tons of sand and gravel, cement and iron must have been put to use here! The controller of an oversight office gives us a number that sums up the gravel used from just one heap. Only after the war will such figures give a concept of the tremendous achievement that the German Reichsbahn, with the help of the French railroads, carried out to prepare for the perhaps decisive battle in the West, which is going on now . . ."

Reichsbahn War Correspondent Bandelow

From the lines in the West, more and more frequently after low-flying Allied attacks, came reports of shots through the boilers of locomotives. To help this situation, efforts were being made to secure the locomotives by partial armor and build protective boxes for the personnel. Some trains were even being equipped with anti-aircraft guns, mostly 2-cm Flak 38 quads. The heavy railroad Flak, a special unit of the *Luftwaffe*, armed mainly with Type 38 and 39 10.5-cm guns, protected the most important railroad objectives.

Borissov, autumn 1941: on the way to a prisoner-of-war assembly camp.

One of 50,000 kilometers: not far from Kiev, railroad engineers lay new rails. October 1941.

Under full sail on the railway: near Kharkov, supplies roll along a broad-gauge line, driven forward by the wind. November 1941.

Personnel transport cars, equipped as required, with floorboards and stoves, seen near Sarny in the late autumn of 1941.

Vyasma, November 1941: a transport train of the *Luftwaffe* uses stakeside cars.

An appeal for partisan warfare, 1941.

Between Vitebsk and Orsha, November 1941: a destroyed German hospital train was tipped on its side to make the tracks usable right away.

Bobruysk, December 1941: a heavy Russian freight locomotive in a hopeless fight with nature.

December 1941, at Stolp depot, Pomerania: the frozen brake couplings have to be thawed out.

Everyday work by the eastern railroad men: radom depot during the severe winter of 1941.

January 1942: a blue railroad man has just oiled the drive rod of his former Prussian state railway locomotive.

On the line from Mogilev to Ostpovici, New Year 1942: a freight-train locomotive from Imperial Russian times works its way slowly ahead.

Eastern front, north sector, winter 1941-42: at a stopping place of Field Railroad Command (FEKdo) 3.

5

The events on the eastern front made clear how much the German military leadership had failed to recognize the role of the railroad. Soon Moltke's old rule of thumb, that military operations run into difficulties when they are more than 100 kilometers away from the end of the railroad, had proved itself.

How right Moltke was also showed itself later in the behavior of the Russians, who had planned and carried out their retreat masterfully. The machines in the railroad plants and workshops had been moved out and transported eastward. Power plants, turntables, and water stations had been blown up. The extent of the destruction was even added to by the German troops, who tore down kilometers of telephone lines, burned snow fences, and loaded spare parts as scrap iron to be sent homeward.

The mobile warfare of the Red Army was also planned around the railroad, and not only for reasons of limited technology. In their retreat, the landing activities of the troops always took place along the high-performance railway lines. Their destruction and removal were planned so that the enemy's later supplying along the same lines would be damaged decisively. The directive of the People's Commissars of the USR and the ZK of the KPdSU of June 29, 1941, reads:

> "*In the forced retreat of the units of the Red Army, the rolling stock of the railroads is to be taken along; neither a locomotive nor a car is to be left behind for the enemy.*"

The Soviets lost only 15% of their locomotives, and thus could save so many cars that throughout the war, even in critical times, they always had a reserve.

Most of the locomotives captured by the Germans were worn out from overly heavy demands and faulty care. They often broke down with some sort of damage on the way from the roundhouse to the cars. Single trains often had to be hauled over short distances by four or five spare locomotives, because one or more would break down from bad coal, air pump, water pump, axle bearing, and similar damage, or the effects of frost.

The rolling stock—locomotives, railcars, and freight and passenger cars, track service cars, and others—were taken along by the Soviets on their retreat, and the long bridges over the Dniepr at Kiex, Kanev, Kremenchug, Dniepropetrovsk, and Saparoshe, over the Narva at Pleskov, and the Bug at Golta and Trichaty were blown up. Until the river crossings were usable again after weeks and months, the goods had to be laboriously reloaded on broad-gauge cars on the other shore, usually by motor vehicles of ferries. In Kiev, to be sure, there were modern signal boxes and electric locomotives, but they were exceptions. Locomotive repair shops and workshops were generally obsolete.

The roadbeds of the Soviet rail lines—usually made of sand, gravel, or crushed stone—and the ties, rails, and so-called small iron were very weak. The ties were made of untreated softwood, and the rails were too light. Thus, only light German locomotives with an axle pressure of up to sixteen tons could usually be used on these tracks, and such were usually old, low-power types that had already been used in World War I.

When possible, every damaged or burned-out freight car was repaired; on the old chassis of freight cars, new bodies were built, creating a new type of car that was marked with a yellow stripe. These "yellow-stripe cars" usually formed complete trains and transported building material, sugar beets, and fertilizer.

At the end of 1942 the rail network in the German-occupied part of the Soviet Union reached its greatest extent of 41,000 kilometers. In Germany there were some 79,000 kilometers; in the present-day Federal Republic fewer than 30,000 kilometers.

Their use, though, was hard to keep going, because the front had meanwhile extended almost 1000 kilometers away from the German border, and they were not prepared to conquer such a distance.

In the time of the greatest unleashing of power—the occupied regions had covered almost five times the extent of the Reich—grain transports from the East also ran to Germany from September 1942 on. In November 1942, when the rail network spread to the suburbs of Stalingrad, to Voronesh and the Terek, the DRB rail lines had a total length of 161,000 kilometers, with 1.7 million railroad officials and workers in gray and blue uniforms to run them. The hotly contested Stalingrad was the easternmost point that the German railroaders reached.

But the cooperation between the blue railroaders and the gray railroad engineers was anything but smooth. The engineers stressed doing fast work and reporting high numbers to their superiors, while the blue railroad men thought of an extended lasting service, with double-track lines if possible. Thus, the gray engineers usually converted only one track of double-track lines and scarcely noticed that loading ramps, locomotive roundhouses, and other important facilities could no longer be reached.

There was also a big problem with Russian schistose coal. It formed a closed, glass-hard cover that had to be torn apart frequently, half a dozen times on a short run. To get by, they loaded wood into the tender. Often, though, the supply had to be replenished at stations or along the tracks, wherever firewood could be found, thus forty hours of travel time for 100 kilometers was not a rarity.

"The German *Reichsbahn* must, above all, transport the goods necessary to the war and to life, and can therefore not satisfactorily handle heavy passenger traffic at Christmas and New Year's. Therefore it asks urgently that between December 20 and January 4 all not absolutely necessary travel, especially on fast and express trains, be given up, and during this time vacation and pleasure trips as well as sports travel be eliminated or limited to short trips.

For certain trains, limited numbers of permission tickets will again be given out without charge at ticket booths and travel agencies."

DNB, December 15, 1942

The condition of the facilities in the East, especially for repairs, care, and maintenance of locomotives, was very meager. Water containers, water towers, and pumps were removed or blown up, likewise power motors. The firemen had to shovel coal unto the tender with shovels, sometimes over makeshift platforms. Even water for the locomotive was often no longer available and had to be brought long distances. The railroad personnel turned old tank cars into makeshift water towers to hold water.

Donetz coal was also a big problem. Only by chance, by inspecting an originally unrecognizable apparatus at the depot in the town of Losovaya, did the railroaders discover that Donetz coal had to be soaked in oil for use in locomotives.

Despite the spreading war, the DRB received only material and industrial capacity for carrying out the most vitally important *Reichsbahn* program, which was based completely on the demands of the *Wehrmacht*. The enduring transport difficulties grew into a serious crisis in the unusually severe winter of 1941-42. The stranding of freight trains added up to 1100 trains in a single day. Totally impossible deliveries and a lack of coal supplies for numerous businesses were the results. By the end of February 1942, 143 armament industries had shut down completely and 35 others partially. In May 1942 it was found that not only the coldness and the freight yards on the eastern front had contributed to the winter crisis. In fact, the *Reichsbahn* was no longer able to meet the demands of the war. Only then did the government deal seriously with the transport problems and change the conditions for the DRB.

Early in June 1942, the Reich Minister for Armament and Ammunition, Albert Speer, got involved.

Albert Speer wrote in his memoirs: "At the same time, Hitler decided that Field Marshal Milch and I should work as traffic dictators temporarily; we should make sure that the demands made 'would be fulfilled to a wide extent and in the shortest time.'"

Albert Ganzenmueller, a strict party member, was, after General Manager Julius Dorpmueller, the second man at the head of the *Reichsbahn*. With the determination that "the war would not be lost because of the transport question" and the order that this question "was to be solved," Hitler ended the important meeting.

Albert Speer commented: "A week after the appointment of Ganzenmueller, on whom such lapidary words about the solution of the transport question had fallen, I visited Hitler again. True to my concept that the leadership had to set examples in critical times, I suggested to Hitler that the use of salon cars by the dignitaries of the Reich and the party be halted until further notice, whereby I naturally was not thinking of himself. But Hitler avoided the decision, in that he maintained that salon cars were necessary in the East because of the poor lodging possibilities. I informed him that most of the cars were not used in the East, but in the Reich, and gave him a long list of countless prominent users of salon cars. But I had no success."

The repairing of locomotives increased from 600 to 1500 machines per month. The likewise increased capacities of the car-building works allowed the number of damaged cars to be reduced from 67,000 in May 1942 to half of that (31,000) in July 1942. The transport situation actually relaxed in the summer of 1942 because of numerous measures. The newly established transport leadership positions assured the best possible utilization of cars. The formerly customary here-and-there movement of the freight cars through half of Europe was limited.

In the Soviet Union, a first of several field railroad directions, later called field railroad commands, was established. Their personnel, the gray railroad men, were subordinate, as military formations, to the chief of Transport, and were the first to reach and work in the captured territories. The field railroaders wore field-gray military uniforms and worked exclusively in the interests of the *Wehrmacht*.

The "Field Railroad Departments," each with a strength of about 1500 men, were likewise subordinated to the *Wehrmacht* transport chief. Former professional railroad men who had been drafted carried out the direct front service. A "Field Railroad Department" was led by the department commander, to whom, among others, a departmental engineer, an operations engineer, an operations controller, and a series of specialists were assigned for the technical work.

Nightly patrols were made to secure the railroad lines, which were endangered by partisans. Kobryn, December 1941.

Schlobin, January 1942: a partisan band has been reported in the vicinity of a railroad junction point.

Schlobin, January 1942: the war against partisans was waged mercilessly by both sides.

"Scrounging coal in broad daylight": briquet transport in DR freight cars of the Villach type; at right a two-axle freight car of the BMB (the railroad of the so-called Protectorate); Lemberg, January 1942.

Kiev, January 1942: German railroad engineers build a line over the frozen Dniepr river, using blocks of ice.

General Government, spring 1942: increased partisan danger!! A warning to travelers from the *Ostbahn* headquarters in Warsaw.

Achtung!

Bei plötzlichem Halt infolge Gleissprengung sofort hinlegen, da Feuerüberfall zu erwarten!

Ferner werden die Fahrgäste im eigenen Interesse dringend gebeten, zwischen und unter den Bänken und Polstersitzen, sowie hinter den Heizkörpern nach versteckten Sprengkörpern, Säureflaschen u. Brandsätzen zu suchen. Verdächtige Gegenstände nicht berühren!

Feststellungen sofort an Eisenbahnbedienstete melden!

Verdächtige Personen festhalten!

Ostbahndirektion
Warschau

Orsha, February 1942: this apparatus on a protective car was supposed to release staff mines with its rod, to protect the locomotive and train from bomb damage.

As in the good old days, a dreamy atmosphere is created by the travel service leader's little house at the Samostotshe depot, February 1942.

At the forest base near Novogrudok, December 1941: a small Diesel locomotive of the German field railways.

March 1942, near Krementchug: opening the 1000-meter Dniepr bridge.

March 1942: an undamaged railroad bridge over the Samoshi at Sathmar, Hungary; a *Wehrmacht* transport with a DR Series 57[10] locomotive.

At the Lichaya depot near Rostov, May 1942: a field-gray railroader reports train arrivals.

Verkehrsstelle

Abfertigung von Truppentransporten,
Wehrmachtgut in Wagenladungen,
Verwundeten- und Gefallenengepäck,
Ladeaufsicht, Wagendienst,
Wagenermittlungsdienst,
Zugabfertigung.

In the first spring sunshine, two railroad men, a blue and a gray, pose for the camera in front of their office entrance at the Kharkov depot, March 1942.

The daily run to the Gomel depot, April 1942: a field-gray railroader turns the signal levers.

May 1942, north of Rostov: a makeshift bridge built in the territory of Field Railroad Command (FEKdo) 5, with a Type HF 110 C narrow-gauge locomotive.

Finland, spring 1942: this improvised armored train guards an important line from partisan attacks.

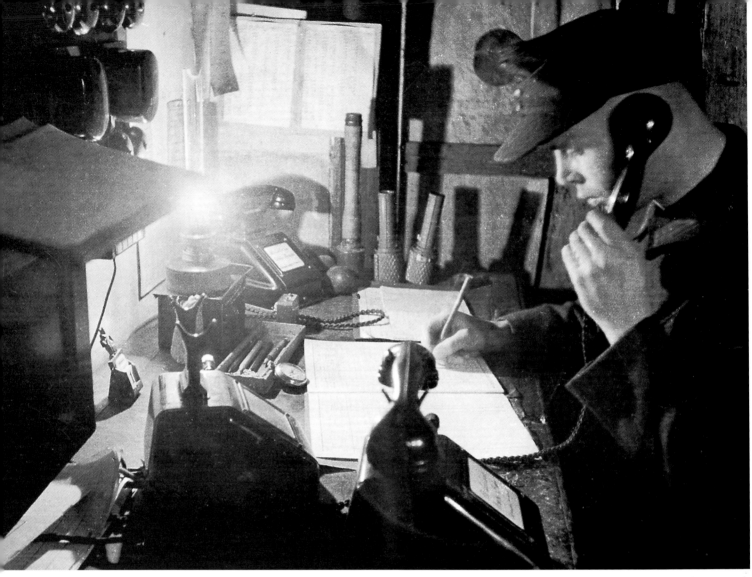

Kazinovici near Gomel, a small depot in the midst of partisan country, June 1, 1942: the work of the railroaders can mean death; hand grenades are ready for use.

Kazinovici near Gomel, June 4, 1942: after the attack, five railroad men are dead, two trains are blown up, and the signal mechanism is destroyed.

Shmerinka, west of Odessa, on the afternoon of July 25, 1942: a makeshift signaling apparatus out in the open, and a former Russian railroad man is there.

1. Fahrzeuge	
	Ölkanne жестянка для масла sheßtjanka dlja mal.
	Handlampe ручная лампа rutschnaja lampa
	Oberwagenlaterne задний сигнал sadnij ßignal

	Petroleumkanne
	жестянка
	     для керосина
	sheßtjanka
	     dlja keraßina

A page from the "Instructions for Communication with Russian Personnel."

A trip without a return: with a locomotive from Imperial times and music, they steam toward their fate. Three young soldiers of the 94th Infantry Division on the line from Tchir to Stalingrad, the easternmost point reached by the German railroad. August 6, 1942.

6

The fast taking of territory in the Soviet Union soon required additional railroad personnel, who were taken directly from the ranks of the DRB. Via very primitive training camps in Deblin and Legionovo in occupied Poland, these men went to serve on the eastern front. They wore blue uniforms and a yellow armband with *"Deutsche Wehrmacht"* lettering. In a letter to the Traffic Minister on November 6, 1941, the Transport Chief complained that the blue railroaders arrived at the front without the needed equipment, sometimes even without eating utensils. As "Wehrmacht followers" they were subordinate to the Transport Chief, but they often encountered the ignorance of the *Wehrmacht*, which was basically responsible for the supplying of the "blue ones."

Even in the field railroad commands, the railroaders were often disrespected for their civilian status and their ranks, which were based on their specialized knowledge. Only in January 1942 did the blue railroaders cease to be "Wehrmacht followers." But this also ended their supplying by the *Wehrmacht*, just as they were slowly beginning to fit in. The railroad men now felt rightfully that they were treated as second-class persons.

For the military trains themselves there was a fixed organization. Supplies traveled on so-called transport routes, which were marked by various colors as in Germany. The red transport route of Wirballen—Kovno—Vilna—Duenaburg—Rositten—Pleskau—Luga—Leningrad ran through the Riga district. Between the transport routes there were connections that could be used in case of disturbances. The military principle was that a high-performance rail line, which must be connected with at least two backland lines parallel to the front, should lead to every army. In the Minsk district, for example, there were even seven such transport routes.

The distances in the occupied part of the USSR were so great that it often took days before the trains reached their destinations. The *Wehrmacht* thus did not know exactly where the individual transports were. But the commanders not only wanted to know how many transports were underway, but on which transport routes they were running.

At the upper train administration in Kiev a really imaginative idea came up: for every train there would be a particular map, and for every run between two locomotive changing depots there would be a box of maps, which held the maps of all the trains that were then on that stretch of track. At two-hour intervals—the trains took that long, on an average, to run between the individual reporting points—the maps corresponding to the incoming reports were put into the next box.

The Reich Travel Directon in Minsk used a map with stickpins for this purpose. The work staff of this, the largest upper train leadership of the DRB, consisted of a leader, his deputy, three representatives each of the southwest and northwest districts, four locomotive service officials, and three workers for the *Illustrated Train Oversight*.

The Minsk district had an extent of some 600 square kilometers. The many sabotage attacks and related, sometimes long-term line or track blockages and unloading limits, plus the often-necessary destination changes in the routing, required the fastest rerouting measures. On the oversight map, six square meters in size, on the wall, the district's nine transport routes were marked by different-colored cords, the different types of trains by colored flags, on pins, in all possible colors, matching the expected line routing.

Every train that was taken over from the district of a neighboring field railroad administration or formed within the district was given a flag, except for the scheduled passenger or freight trains that were already kept track of. The trains passing through were marked daily, at every passage, in the planned daily schedule to the right and left of the oversight map. From the point of being taken over, they moved to their turnover or dissolution on the basis of the eight-hour reports of the train leadership, on the most favorable lines through the district.

Deviations from the planned route were identifiable immediately by means of the colored pins, which had to agree with the color of the planned route. Thus, despite the changes in time or route caused by enemy activity and accidents, a look at the oversight map sufficed to tell at once whether, where, and when a train was to be sought on a run between two locomotive-changing depots, or at what freight station, storage, or changing depot it was at that time. When a train reached its destination or left the district, its flag was marked with the corresponding arrival entry and kept.

The Gray River on Wheels

"The great central dividing site for military travelers is the 'Friedrichstrase' depot in Berlin. Not by the platform, but by the baggage and equipment, was the destination recognized. To the west there are trunks, stiff service caps, and maybe even a briefcase. For the East, there are large rolls of bedding, stable lanterns, and Primus stoves wrapped in newspaper. Dress boots travel to the west, combat boots to the east. The U-Boat sailor from the Atlantic coast has some wrapped-up sandwiches and travel [Marken] with him, the man on furlough from the East has marching provisions for eight days, a cooking pan and a washbowl. Going west there is usually an individual traveler sitting behind the latest newspaper.

The East requires the formation of groups. One must bring the food, another must guard the baggage when the group is on the move. A third heats the small iron stove until the wooden benches begin to smolder, and a fourth distributes the soup so efficiently that before the departure he can even have the field flasks filled with tea . . .

For this travel too, there are special lists, especially among the couriers and command carriers. For them it is an honor to reach the Caucasian front in four or five days while newcomers are still waiting for connections in Bataisk. They have a special sense for special trains or coupled-on cars. They have already traveled in a bed of an empty hospital train and in the map room of a commander. They climb onto the bomb crates of an ammunition train as onto a locomotive running alone to test a new track . . .

They are a kind of 'record tramps' of the great iron army road. Their honor consists of speed, and whoever wants to tell them something of travel techniques just inspires a broad smile . . ."

Reichsbahn, 3-4 1942.

Because of the heavy demands on the railroad personnel, a furlough ban had to be applied in December 1941. The situation continued to get worse. Water cranes, containers, and pipes that were not buried at least two meters deep in the ground froze solid.

Then there was no water, for the ground-water table sank and the sources dried up. Further problems for train traffic were caused by snowdrifts in the woodless regions of the Ukraine.

At the beginning of January 1942, temperatures fell to 45 degrees below zero. Under the tremendous pressure of strong Soviet groups, the German troops had to retreat to defensible positions. On the front lines there were shortages of gasoline, ammunition, and provisions. On February 4, 1942, the traffic of Railroad Command 3 was completely halted. On the most important line, Brest-Litovsk—Minsk—Smolensk, only eight trains a day made it through in February 1942; the others were backed up to the Gedob district and filled the sidetracks.

The strong cold snap in January 1942 had bad effects not only on the eastern front, but on the entire Reich. The frost reduced the reserve equipment to a minimum. The German locomotives were fully unsuitable for the long cold spells. Their exposed piston-feeding pumps and injectors, preheaters, and all exposed oil and water lines were too sensitive to frost. The lack of lubrication led to hot axle bearings. The steam pumps of the German locomotives were also too delicate and far less sturdy than the Russian ones. Since there were too few roundhouses and locomotive sheds, the engine situation became a problem. Locomotives had to be thawed outdoors with open fires. Water cranes froze and controls iced up. Accidents piled up, since signal lights were often stolen. Hospital trains needed a second locomotive, as no heater cars were available.

The Central *Reichsbahn* Office in Berlin sent out instructions on November 27, 1941, to tell how locomotives could be protected from frost. They recommended the use of light wooden boxes around the endangered pumps. The pipes on locomotives of the same type were also not uniformly located. As for the exposed oil lines, the Central Office thought they could be wrapped with paper cord and then given a coating of tar.

Only at the end of February 1942, when the worst part of the winter was almost over, did new instructions for a "*final frost-protection equipping*" come from Berlin. Even the locomotives newly arriving from Germany were no longer usable beyond Brest-Litovsk because of frost damage. Thawing sheds, at which ice and snow could be melted off after the locomotives were used, were almost completely lacking. The machines could be thawed only in the servicing pits of the factories.

The hard winter also meant danger for the makeshift bridges over rivers, especially at the beginning of the spring thaw. In April 1942 the flood waters of the Vorskla, a tributary of the Dniepr, flooded the Poltava depot and the housing of Field railroad Command 3. The floods washed away the rails at the depot and caused the railroad bridge 40 kilometers to the south, on the line to Krementschlug, to collapse. It could not be decided who was responsible for protecting the endangered bridges.

On March 6, 1942, when a representative of the Reich Traffic Ministry examined the Duena bridge on the Polotsk-Duenaburg line, nobody could tell him who was responsible for protecting this important bridge: the engineer staff, the *Reichsbahn* building troop of HBD North on Riga, the Special Bridge Office of HBD Center in Minsk, or the Polotsk traffic office.

By this time, 70% of the locomotives had broken down, even 80% of the standard-gauge machines, and 60% of the broad-gauge engines of Field Railroad Command 3 in Kiev. The Minsk operations office could only operate ten of a hundred locomotives, and even that was troublesome.

Memories for Postwar Times

"It is intended that after the war ends, the war activity of the German Reichsbahn should be portrayed in an inclusive presentation and thus devoted to a considerable part of the experiences of the railroad men in the various theaters of war and dangerous service in the homeland. Since such experience reports can be gathered only after the war ends and thus will lack the immediacy and closeness of their experiences, reducing the vigor of many interesting details in their memories, the collection of suitable material, organized by service districts, should be assured now . . . The reports should not be prepared according to an established pattern; excerpts from daybooks and letters can be especially valuable. Humor should also have its rightful place."

NSBZ-Voraus, 18-19, 1942

The building of 1350 steam locomotives and 65,000 cars planned for 1940 could not be accomplished, because repairing and rebuilding work required more raw materials than could be assigned for this purpose. Only at the end of 1942 did Hitler realize what value the railroads, much ignored by him until then, had for the administration and use of the occupied territories. The backlog should be made up by increased deliveries, for it was clear that the DRB was not able to meet the demands of the war with the equipment they had at that time. Thinking that the armed conflict would be settled soon, the DRB originally was not given any noteworthy priorities. Only from 1941 on was it finally included in the armament plans. Now they tried to produce as many robust war locomotives as possible in the shortest time.

At a special conference, important decisions were made for the *Reichsbahn*. Speer was entrusted with carrying out the "F'hrer Program," by which the building of 15,000 war locomotives in a time period of two years was to be accomplished.

A. Speer noted in his memoirs: "When Göring heard that we intended to expand locomotive production, he had me come to Karinhall. He seriously suggested to me that locomotives be built of concrete, since we did not have enough steel on hand. The concrete locomotives would, of course, not last as long as the steel ones, he thought, but one would simply have to build correspondingly more locomotives. Of course he did not know how that was to be done; yet he harped for months on this deviant idea, for which I spent two hours driving, two hours waiting, and brought home an empty stomach."

The Reich Traffic Ministry had a committee check the suggestions for simplifying the design of Series 50 locomotives. And in December 1941 they wanted to know from the applicable industrial firms to what extent they were capable of producing a suitable new locomotive. According to the Ministry's view, these locomotives, with a saving of material and production time, should be able to pull 1200-ton trains at a speed of at least 65 kph with the same axle load (15 Mp) as the Series 50 type.

These simplified locomotives were to bear the letters ÜK (Übergangs-Kriegslokomotive = temporary war locomotives) after their service numbers. All locomotive factories were to become partners in the Union of Great-German Locomotive Factories (GGL). A reorganization plan foresaw the end of Series 44 and 86 production in May 1943. The production of Series 50 should begin with 65 units in January 1942 and be expanded to 620 simplified Series 52 war locomotives by June 1943. On August 15, 1942, the contract for 15,000 locomotives, probably the largest in Central European locomotive construction, was issued to the industry. It foresaw the building of 7000 locomotives of Series 52 — deliverable by February 1944 — and 8000 of the already planned but not yet completely designed Series 42.

The first designs for the second war locomotive (Series 42) went back to 1941. On advice from the *Ostbahn*, the Polish Ty 37 locomotive was chosen as the design model. On the basis of this beginning, the DRB was for the first time assigned steel in hitherto unknown quantities. In the third quarter of 1942, the industry received 69,500 tons of raw steel per month for building locomotives. In all, 6575 Series 52 units were built by Henschel, Borsig, Krauss-Maffei, and MBA in Germany, and also by Skoda in Czechoslovakia and Chrzanov in Poland. On March 7, 1942, there was an agreement between Speer and Dorpmueller that building vehicles for the *Reichsbahn* was to be integrated into the whole armament industry. Thus, locomotive building became part of armament building and was first prioritized according to its importance.

"52001" in Field Gray—The War Created its Locomotives

"The German soldier has received a new field-gray comrade: the war locomotive. In many ways the same fate links them. Just as he has always accepted the hard necessities of the war, from which he gains experience and goes into battle more knowledgeable and experienced every day, thus in this total war the development in all areas, especially in technology, is constantly in flux. Nobody will assert that the locomotives that were built in Germany to date are bad. But they were, as the Fuehrer declared in his Reichstag speech on April 26, like the German people, not prepared for the degree of coldness that overwhelmed us in the winter fighting of 1941-42.

Every soldier who wears the red order ribbon has experienced that; he knows how tough and extensive the service and also the wear on locomotives was in the East. Every breakdown of a locomotive, though, creates a tangible gap in our activity, especially at a time in which the growing demands constantly require more rolling stock.

One need only see the vast areas on the map that have been conquered and occupied by our troops to imagine what traffic achievements are necessary to assure supplying the *Wehrmacht*.

That is why the new war locomotive was created. It is winter-tough, so it can stand even the eastern coldness. Its production also requires significantly less time and material. In the first model, including the tender, some 26,000 kilograms of material could be saved and the building time reduced by 6000 work hours. Success that was attained in a short time will have their full effect only when—after a transitional series, which is being built now—the production program begins on January 1, 1943. The first locomotive of the new Series 52, which will thus bear number 52001, is already finished and has covered 5000 kilometers, including the most difficult tracks with steep mountain stretches, sharp bends and insufficient roadbeds, passing the test for its later service, which will occur particularly in the East.

Its field-gray color is more than a symbol. For like the soldier, who has dealt with everything that burdens him, it has been the same for it. The specialist speaks of 'refinement.' For example, the paint finish was spared, unnecessary polish eliminated, the whistle and wind deflectors omitted. But extra weight was devoted to frost protection. And here the non-expert can also tell the new type from the former one. The steam and water pipes are moved as much as possible under the boiler covering, all the others are given warmth shielding by pipe jackets. The oil lines for cylinder lubrication are jacketed and fitted with heating. For just as weapons must remain in operation despite heavy frost, so it must be assured that the oil in the axles and shafts of the 'loco' will not stiffen and freeze. In the new locomotive, the smokestack flap is especially sensitive. Whoever remembers the oldest locomotives will greet an old acquaintance in this flap. On the war locomotive it is closed when the 'loco' is not in operation, to keep the machinery from cooling. But the driver and his comrade, the fireman, have also been thought of. They will no longer be exposed, as they were last winter, to the icy windstream that makes every hour of bearing it a tough test of will. The cab is now completely covered by a wooden shell, connected to the tender by a canvas bellows. The floor of the cab is also warmed by a heating coil. There are also numerous other frost-protecting measures that only the locomotive expert needs to deal with. Let it just be noted that the capacities of the water tanks of the war locomotive were increased to 34 cubic meters from the previous 26 cubic meters. More coal can also be carried, ten tons instead of the former eight.

From childhood on, man is especially fond of the 'iron horse.' How very different for the soldier! For him, the German locomotive is a bit of homeland that comes to him, loyal and reliable, over thousands of kilometers that separate him from home. The homeland sends the war locomotive to him in the field as a new comrade, the 'protection loco.' And this 'protection loco' will be a loyal image of the soldier, just as reliable in every situation, modest and unassuming, just as tough and durable when it needs to be, and always ready to pull even the most stranded cars out of the dirt."
Die Wehrmacht, 1942

To make the new locomotive suit the war requirements better, Hitler requested: "In the East locomotives, a toilet pipe in simplest form should be installed quickly, plus a spotlight operable from the cab by a turnable ball-joint." This was not done.

The first regular war locomotive, 52001, was displayed to the public on September 12, 1942, and then began a propaganda trip through Germany. According to plan, the German locomotive factories set their goal—the building of 500 units per month—for the early summer of 1943. This goal was first attained in June 1943. But in March 1943, Hitler promised his generals that tank production would be doubled. Now Speer had to give priority to carrying out the "Adolf Hitler Tank Program," and locomotive production slid down from the highest priority of armament production.

"In recognition of the unique achievements of the railroaders in this war, I declare that the 7th of December is the Day of the German Railroader."

Adolf Hitler, December 7, 1943

"Professional comrades, my guests! Why have we chosen December 7 as the Day of the German Railroader? Because on December 7, 108 years ago, the first German train covered the short stretch from Nuernberg to Fuerth. From the few men who drove that train, there has grown the tremendous number of 1,600,000 railroaders. Every 18th man in the German Reich is a railroader or belongs to a railroader's family . . . When we defy all difficulties and observe the first Day of the German Railroader in the fifth war year, this shall be our thanks to all railroaders for their achievements in this war time. They have passed the test of fire; the requirements of the *Wehrmacht* are fulfilled, the needs of the armament industry were met and the supplying of the German people by transport assured . . ."

Reich Traffic Minister Dorpmueller

Exact figures on the achievements of the DRB in the military sector can no longer be determined, as documents were destroyed, but one can assume that in Germany some 70% and the occupied Soviet area some 90% of the trains were operated by it.

THE NEW WAR LOCOMOTIVE

"In March of this year, the Führer informed the Reich Minister for Armament and Ammunition that locomotive and railroad car production was to be included in the armament program and increased. Within this operation, a new war locomotive was developed, which brought *considerable material savings* through simplification of production. Further, through the thus introduced simplification of production in six months 1,150,000 *work hours were saved*. According to the results to date, it is to be expected that the goal set by the Fuehrer will be not only reached but *far exceeded* in a short time.

The work is being done by the main branch for rail vehicles at the Reich Ministry for Armament and Ammunition, Speer, whose leader is Director Gerhard Degenkolb. Press representatives were offered the opportunity to see this Series 52 war locomotive and, with it, a train unit comprising six freight cars and two baggage cars.

This *simplified locomotive design,* which is the only type built in very large numbers by all Great German locomotive factories for the Reichsbahn, is a joint project by the Union of Great German Locomotive Factories. For the war locomotive including tender, an estimated 26,000 kilograms of material and 6000 work hours per locomotive are saved. Some 12,000 kg are saved in the tender, the weight of which could be decreased from 26 to 18 tons, yet it now can carry 34 cubic meters of water instead of the previous 26, and 10 instead of 8 tons of coal.

From the clarifications given out by the leader of the main branch, Director Degenkolb, the extensive simplification of types was especially illuminating. The number of steam locomotive types was reduced from 119 to 12, that of fireless types from 11 to 2, that of motor locomotives from 97 to 5, and that of various motors from 74 to 4. These simplifications have led to the aforementioned saving of work time, and what that means under present conditions will be clear to everyone. The *simplifications* do not extend only to locomotive construction, but also include the illustrated *freight cars.* Thus the present design of baggage cars (Pwgs) has been reduced by 25 vH, the covered freight cars (Glhs) by 38 vH, and the (G) from 24 to 30 vH or 45 to 50 vH,

depending on the load weight. For the uncovered freight cars (Ghs), the saving is 29 or 49 vH, for refrigerator cars 34.4 or 50.6 vH, for stakeside cars (Rmms) 24 or 63 vH, and open freight cars (Ommu) 29.3 or 33.3 vH, depending on the load weight. One must imagine these great savings of material and work time on the one hand, and the tremendous need for rail vehicles on the other, to gain the right concept of the significance of these measures.

In locomotive construction, the saving of work time from April 1 to September 1, 1942 has led to a *production increase* of 92.5 vH. Thus in September almost twice as many locomotives have been delivered by the factories as in March of this year. The further measures introduced since then and still being implemented, such as the time process—thus does the specialist call the assembly-line work fitted to the needs of locomotive production—will lead to a *considerable further saving* within a year.

The financial and material side should not be overlooked either, for the larger the delivery is, the greater is the saving in material and the possibility of its use elsewhere, as well as the decrease in the cost of producing individual locomotives. The displayed train unit has proved itself splendidly in a trip of over 5000 kilometers, on which the decisive loading influences were sought. What speaks especially for the goodness of the design is the proving of chassis that can in no way be compared with those of the German *Reichsbahn.* Thus the necessary safety is provided for the demands that the *Reichsbahn* must place on its rolling stock.

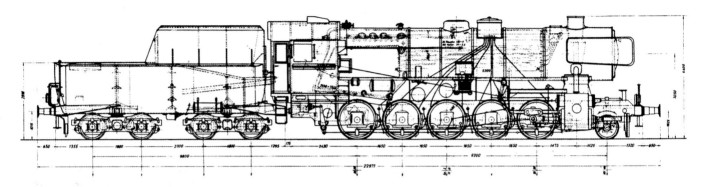

Autumn 1942: war freight locomotive, Series 52: enclosed on all sides, double-walled cab, plus boiler insulated with fiberglass matting.

Technical Data: BR 52, Borsig, sheet-metal frame, built in 1942

Price with tender 2'2'T 30m autumn 1942	179,000 RM
Axle sequence	1'E h2
Speed (maximum)	80/80 kph
Drive-wheel diameter	850 mm
Axle interval (firm)	3300 mm
Total axle wheelbase (without tender)	9200 mm
Length from buffers (with tender)	22,975 mm
Weight empty	75.9 tons
Weight in service	84.0 tons
Tender 2'2'T 30 (empty)	18.7 tons
Friction weight	75.7 Mp
Maximum axle load	15.4 Mp
Cylinder diameter	600 mm
Piston stroke	660 mm
Boiler pressure	16 atu
Rust surface	3.89 sq.m.
Radiating heat surface	15.9 sq.m.
Pipe heat surface	161.93 sq.m.
Length of pipes	5200 mm
Long diameter of boiler	1700 mm
Boiler water capacity	7.75 cub.m.
Steam space	3.00 cub.m.
Steaming surface	10.80 sq.m.
Overheater heating surface	66.94 sq.m.
Cited steam production	10.1 t.h.
Indexed power	1620 HP
Indexed pulling power	21,720 kg

The exact number of Series 52 steam locomotives produced until the collapse of the Third Reich can no longer be determined, but amounts to approximately 6500 units. The Series 52, conceived as a design purely for wartime purposes with a limited lifetime, proved thanks to its simple, solid construction to be a truly long-lasting machine. Except for Britain, the Iberian Peninsula, Switzerland and Sweden, it performed its daily service in Western and Eastern Europe, including the Soviet Union, until the 1970s. It was still built for some years after the war in Belgium, Luxembourg, and Poland. And who is fortunate can still see it performing its service in East European countries today. The Series 52 is also, except for the [text missing], the most often-built locomotive series in the world.

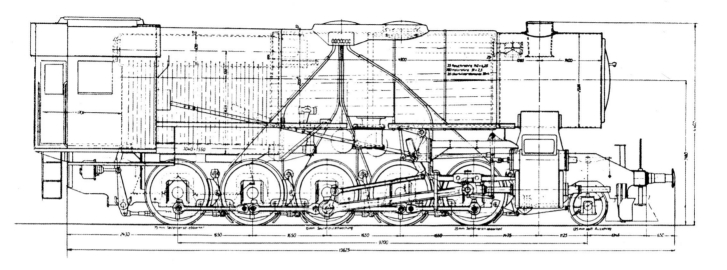

August 1943, second war locomotive, Series 42: Henschel and Viennese Locomotive Factory, with steel frame and [Brotan] boiler, developed after experience with the Polish Ty 37 freight locomotive.

Technical Data: Series 42, Henschel-Florisdorf—WLF, built in 1943 with [Brotan] water-pipe boiler (+ Tender 2'2'T 30)

Price with tender, autumn 1943	155,000 RM
Axle interval	1'E h2
Speed (maximum)	80/80 kph
Carrying-wheel diameter	850 mm
Drive-wheel diameter	1400 mm
Axle wheelbase (fixed)	3300 mm
Total axle wheelbase (without tender)	9200 mm
Length from buffers (with tender)	23,000 mm
Weight empty	90,0 tons
Weight in service	99.6 tons
Tender 2'2'T 30 mm (empty)	46.0 tons
Friction weight	88.8 Mp
Maximum axle load	18.3 Mp
Cylinder diameter	630 mm
Piston stroke	660 mm
Boiler pressure	16 atu.
Rust surface	4.71 sq.m.
Radiating heat surface	20.85 sq.m.
Pipe heating surface	190.14 sq.m.
Length of pipes	4900 mm
Long diameter of boiler	2000 mm
Boiler water capacity	9.25 cub.m.
Steam space	3.70 cub.m.
Steaming surface	10.48 sq.m.
Overheater heat surface	71.20 sq.m.
Cited steam production	ca. 13 t/h
Indexed performance	V 1800 HP
Indexed pulling power	23,960 kg

Some 900 Series 42 locomotives were built by the war's end. They were conceived with design and production-technology savings, and also under consideration of the poor track situation in Eastern Europe. The robust Series 42 freight locomotive is still used today in some East European countries. Some 120 units have been built in Poland since 1950.

August 1942: the bridge at Krivoy-Rog, rebuilt with the cooperation of Hungarian railroad engineers, with a brand new Series 424 locomotive.

Ukraine, summer 1942: fifteen kilometers from Vinniza, on the line to Schitomir, is Hitler's new "Werewolf" headquarters train. The two big shots, Himmler and Bormann, are seen on the makeshift platform, with a salon wagon in the background.

Kiev, summer 1942: a refrigerator car from Silesia with specialties for the officers' canteen.

Lower left: the work of German railroad engineers, a bridge over the Selm near Konotop, summer 1942. Again a G 10 locomotive.

Right: summer 1942, eastern front, southern sector: every rebuilt bridge is put in service, a joyous day for the assembled railroad engineers.

From "Voelkischer Beobachter:, 7/8/1942.

From "Voelkischer Beobachter", 7/1/1942

From "Voelkischer Beobachter", 7/11/1942

From "Voelkischer Beobachter", 7/2/1942

From "Voelkischer Beobachter, 7/29/1942

From "Voelkischer Beobachter", 7/15/1942

From "Voelkischer Beobachter", 8/6/1942

From "Voelkischer Beobachter", 12/14/1942

Vorbereitung für die Heimat
1. Munition abgeben.
2. Entlausung.
3. Papiere kontrollieren, Zugzuweisung und abstempeln auf Befehlsstand.
4. Marschverpflegung empfangen.
5. Geld wechseln.
6. Je, nach Wunsch zum Verschönerungsrat.
7. Anmeldung daheim durch Post im Lager: „Mutti, ich komme!"
8. Zu den Zügen wird abgerufen, etwa 1½ Std. vorher angetreten und eingeteilt.
9. Alles mit guter Laune, sauberem Benimm und Freude auf die Heimat.

"With good mood and clean behavior": on the way home from the eastern front. Kupyansk, autumn 1942.

NSDAP
Urlauberbetreuung
Pakete des Führers für Frontsoldaten
Ausgabe ←

Kupyansk, east of Kharkov, autumn 1942: on furlough with the *Führer*-package.

Verlauste und Urlauber halt
Meldung im Zelt
20 Schritt zurück.

Tips for railroad passengers on the way home.

Entlausungs-Anstalt

One of the most important services (delousing) at the Brest-Litovsk depot, summer 1942.

Direction sign, Dniepropetrovsk depot, summer 1942.

The first duty of a man on furlough in 1942: turn over ammunition. Gomel, September 1942.

Before the express-train timetable with furlough section (SF trains): three information aides (called "Lightning Girls") at the Rouen main depot, France, September 1942.

On a day in Smolensk, October 1942: the Führer-package.

A seaman goes home: St. Nazaire depot, September 1942.

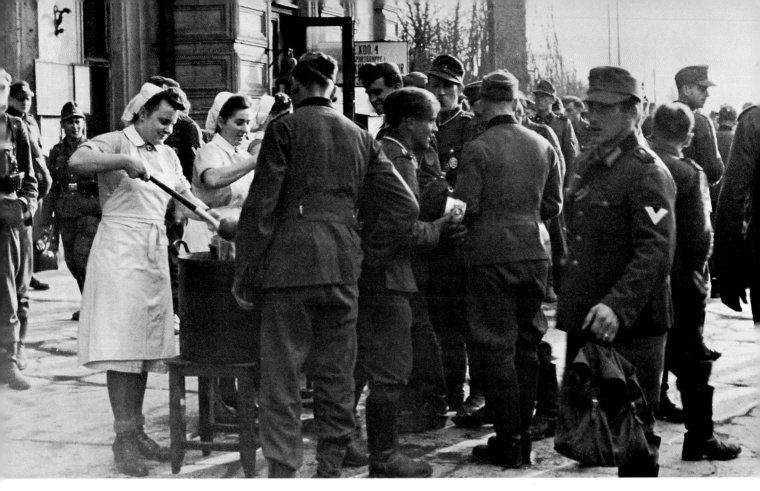

Minsk main depot, August 1942: standing in line to get coffee.

"You will be called to the trains, assembled about ½ hour in advance and divided": a well-earned nap at the Byelogrod depot, September 1942.

An express train with furlough section from Trier to La Negresse via Metz and Bordeaux, September 1942.

"Your furlough ticket, please! ..."

7

Other than the perfectly carried-out advances in the West and East, the mastering of daily supplying for the fighting troops at the theaters of war in all of Europe, the supplying of German and foreign industrial cities and the provisioning of the population, the DRB, despite the constantly increasing difficulties, provided a further, though grim task: carrying dead bodies to death camps. In addition, many thousand "*train movements*" were needed to transport millions of Jews from all parts of the continent to the ovens of Treblinka, Maydanek, or Ahschwitz.

It is obvious that without the silence of the Allies in the East and West the DRB could not master this task. No aircraft disturbed the "*resettlement transports,*" no low-flying plane shot down a locomotive of the death trains, no bomber squadron dropped its destructive load on one of the rail junctions that linked the lines to the extermination camps. The partisans in the woods of Russia, Poland, France, and the Balkans also stayed in their hideouts.

Without this remarkable inactivity by Hitler's opponents, who knew what was going on from the beginning and, in the pursuit of their own strategic goals, knew very definitely how the accomplishments of the DRB were to be destroyed, the initiator of the Final Solution, SS *Obersturmbannfuehrer* Adolf Eichmann, could never have carried out his plan. This is also part of the DRB's wartime annals.

The experience report that Police Captain Fritz Salitter, as commander of an escort command of the Duesseldorf *Gestapo* submitted on December 26, 1941, describes one of those trips from which there was no return.

> "*Confidential!*
> Report on the evacuation of Jews to Riga. Transport escort at strength of 1/15 from 12/11 to 12/17/1941.
> *Course of Transport.* The transportation of Jews from the cities of Duisburg, Krefeld, several small towns and rural districts of the Rhenish-Westphalian industrial area, was planned for 12/11/1941. Duesseldorf was represented by only 19 Jews. The transport consisted of Jews of both sexes and various ages, from infants to age 65.

The departure of the transport was scheduled for 9:30 AM, for which the Jews were already assembled on the loading ramp as of 4:00. The *Reichsbahn* could not provide the train that early, apparently for lack of personnel, so that the loading of the Jews could only be begun around 9:00. The loading was done with the greatest haste, since the *Reichsbahn* insisted on departing according to schedule if possible. . .

On the way from the slaughterhouse to the loading ramp, a male Jew tried to commit suicide by being run over by a streetcar. But he was caught by the bumper of the streetcar and only slightly injured. At first he pretended to be dying, but during the trip he soon became very cheerful when he realized that he could not escape the fate of evacuation.

An old Jewess also left the loading ramp unnoticed, fled into a nearby house, undressed, and sat on a water closet. A cleaning woman noticed her, though, so that she could be taken back to the transport. The loading of the Jews was finished about 10:15. After switching several times, the train then left the Duesseldorf-Derendorf freight station n the direction of Wuppertal around 10:30 . . . After the last switching I found that the car of the escort command (2nd class) had been coupled at the end of the passenger cars, the 21st car, instead of in the middle of the train.

Around 11:10 Konitz was reached. I could carry out my duties except for the relocation of my own car. At first this was promised, but then the station master explained to me that coupling the car in the middle of the train was not possible for lack of a switch engine and the necessary track, but he would have the car moved forward. I agreed to this . . . After about five minutes, though, he came back and explained to me that he had to let the train depart immediately, and that switching was now impossible, with 50 minutes having passed meanwhile.

This behavior of the stationmaster seemed incomprehensible to me, and I therefore had a serious talk with him, saying that I intended to make a complaint to the appropriate oversight office.

He explained to me that this office could not be reached by me, that he had his orders and had to let the train depart at once, because two other trains were expected. He even suggested to me that a car in the middle of the train be cleared of Jews and occupied by my command and the Jews be placed in the second-class escort car. It seemed appropriate to make it clear to this railroad official of important position that he was to treat members of the German Police differently from Jews. I had the impression that it was not proper for him to speak of the 'poor Jews' as if they were comrades, and that the concept of 'Jew' was totally strange to him. This railroad official even managed to let the train depart without its leader, as I had to leave it for two minutes to have a foreign body removed from my eye at the Red Cross station. Only the intervention of one of my sentries was to be thanked for the fact that the locomotive driver, after starting up, stopped again, and I was able to reach the train with difficulty. . . At the Schaulen depot (1:12) the escort team of Red Cross nurses was sufficiently and well fed. Barley broth was followed by beef . . .

At 19:30 Mitau (Latvia) was reached. Here a considerably cooler temperature made itself known. Snow began to fall and frost to form. Arrival in Riga took place at 21:50, where the train was held at the depot for one and a half hours. Here I learned that the Jews were not meant for the Riga ghetto, but were to be housed in the ghetto of Skirotava, 8 km northeast of Riga. At 13:12, after much switching back and forth, the train reached the military ramp at the Skirotava depot. The train remained standing unheated. The outdoor temperature was already 12 degrees below zero.

Turning over the train then took place at 1:45, and at the same time the supervision was taken over by six Latvian policemen. Since it was already past midnight and the loading ramp was very icy, the unloading and the transport of the Jews to the assembly ghetto some two kilometers away could only take place at sunup on Sunday."

signed Salitter, Police Captain

Eichmann's right-hand man, SS *Hauptsturmfuehrer* Dieter Wisliceny, described the method of obtaining trains for deportation quite precisely:

"For the provision of special trains or cars, Eichmann had instructed his traffic officer, SS *Hauptsturmfuehrer* Nowack, who did what was necessary along with Ministerialrat Stange. Local transit situations, though, are worked out between the *Gestapo* on the scene and the responsible Reich railroad direction or the local depot administration."

Since the *Wehrmacht* had a say in the matter, Stange had to get in touch with the military. For the OKW, though, it was only a matter of having a veto power if the *Wehrmacht* was just on the march. Otherwise Hitler banned the support.

Another exchange of letters shows that the Traffic Ministry also took an active part in the Final Solution. The State Secretary of the Reich Traffic Ministry, Ganzenmueller, wrote to Himmler's intimate friend and Chief of the Personal Staff, SS *Obergruppenfuehrer* Karl Wolff, on July 28, 1942:

"Since July 2 a train with 5000 Jews has run from Warsaw via Malkinia to Treblinka, plus twice a week a train with 5000 Jews from Przemysl to Belzec. Gedob is in constant touch with the security service in Krakow."

The reply from Wolff to Ganzenmueller, discovered by the deputy prosecutor at the Nuernberg Trials, Robert Kempner, read:

"Dear Party Member Ganzenmueller! In the name of the *Reichsführer* SS I thank you very much for your letter. I have learned from your communication with great pleasure that for two weeks a train with 5000 of the Chosen People has been running to Treblinka. I have gotten in touch with the participating offices so that all of the measures appear to be carried out without trouble."

The commander of the Auschwitz extermination camp, Rudolf Hoess, also reported:

> "The program of individual actions, which was specified precisely in a schedule discussion by the Reich Traffic Ministry, absolutely had to be maintained to avoid a stoppage of the applicable railroad lines, particularly for military reasons."

From the documents still available it can be seen that the offices assigned to the Reich Traffic Ministry, the General Business Administrations, the *Reichsbahn* Administration, the Gedob, the *Ostbahn* Administrations, the Reich Traffic Authorities in occupied Russia and the *Reichsbahn* offices in the occupied and allied countries received binding instructions. So many offices of the railroad—though it always involved only a small number of people—gained a certain knowledge of the deportation and the destinations from which only empty trains returned. In a totalitarian state it is naturally unthinkable to obstruct such instructions. There was also pressure and surveillance by the local SS offices, especially in the General Government, where the notorious SS and Police Commander Friedrich-Wilhelm Krueger was in charge.

The transports ran under the strictest secrecy. The knowledge that concentration camps were also extermination camps was limited to a certain group of people. In no meeting of the Gedob or the department chief was a word ever said about the transportation of Jews or the extermination camps. The SS for its part only requisitioned the railroad cars by giving trip numbers. The car office never knew for what purpose the cars were actually used. For example, the transports to the Treblinka extermination camp were listed in the schedules as: Special relocation train, special train with workers, Pj special train, special train with relocaters, or DA trains.

The General Administration of the *Ostbahn* in Krakau mentioned in their Schedule Order No. 234 that the Treblinka depot was closed to public traffic indefinitely as of September 1, 1942, "to allow the smooth running of the relocation trains." At the Treblinka depot, though, a cynical idea by camp commander Kurt Franz led to the building of a modern station with all possible features, for the sake of appearances. There were even printed timetables for trains to and from Grodno, Suwalki, Vienna, and Berlin. When the name Treblinka became notorious, the phony depot was given a gigantic sign with the name: "OBERMAYDANEK."

The documents also show that despite everything, efforts were made to interfere with these transports. Even in Polish deportations it was said in police reports that *Reichsbahn* personnel showed little interest, even opposition in part. Yet the railroad fulfilled the tasks it was given. It is the result of confident relations on a high level between Himmler's agency and the *Reichsbahn* leadership.

Przemysl, September 1942: an infantry division on its way to the eastern front.

Autumn 1942: a short rest between Lemberg and Kiev.

Signore, cigarettes …you're welcome: at the Fuscaldo depot, November 1942. In the right background are four-axle Italian passenger cars.

Koenigsberg main depot: destination fo two Red Cross nurses, autumn 1942.

The furlough train has just reached Dole, in the French Jura, autumn 1942.

A little refreshment: the train stops at Poltava, autumn 1942.

Mütter und Kinder werden in nichtluftgefährdete Gebiete umquartiert

Im Aufnahmegau leben die Umquartierten sicher vor feindlichem Luftterror

In der Geborgenheit eines Lagers der Kinderlandverschickung

Die Deutsche Re
sorgt für die Bef
Hunderttausender
gefährdeten Geb
die Aufnahmegau
daran! Reise nur,
dem Siege d

**Ob kurz die Reise oder weit –
Bleibt, wo Ihr wohlgeborgen seid: REIST NICHT!**

Die Deutsche Reichsbahn dient der Kriegführung! Wichtiger als deine Reise ist der Transport
von Rohstoffen für die Rüstungsindustrie
von Lebensmitteln für die Heimat
von Waffen für die Front

Fronturlauber kommen nach Hause

Panzer rollen zur Front

Kartoffelverladung zur Versorgung der städt. Bevölkerung

Kohlenzufuhr für die Rüstung

Autumn 1942: "Travel only when it aids victory!"

Shortly after sunrise on the long track between Smolensk and Baranovici in a makeshift passenger car of the "wooden class," autumn 1942.

Polotsk, autumn 1942: the mixed troop transport train has finally arrived.

At a small station near Beauvais, autumn 1942: the two-axle DR freight car, from the Stettin district, is loaded with captured French ammunition.

On the way between Stuttgart and Bordeaux, autumn 1942.

One becomes thoughtful: on the trip from Frankfurt to the eastern front, autumn 1942.

Opposite: When they still had a lot of time: the gateway arch of Field Railroad Command 4 (FEKdo) on the Pleska-Luga line, autumn 1942.

Three eggs for breakfast in the morning in an improvised building troop dwelling car near Vilna, autumn 1942.

Above left: Time for a chat in the dining car on the line between Paris and Cherbourg in 1942. Commander West, General Field Marshal von Rundstedt, enjoys his cigar. Above right: A side passage in a first-class SNCF passenger car in Field Marshal von Rundstedt's special train, France 1942.

A sleeping car of a special SNCF train for the commander West, autumn 1942: not exactly suited for a telephone switchboard.

On a sidetrack near Cherbourg, autumn 1942: Field Marshal von Rundstedt leaves his special train.

Autumn 1942: a formal reception at a Paris depot.

Räder müssen rollen für den Sieg!

Auf jeden Güterwagen kommt es an für den kriegswichtigen Einsatz in Front und Heimat! Jeder muß mithelfen, um den Güterwagenumlauf zu beschleunigen, Wagenraum zu sparen und Wagenstillstand zu vermeiden!

10 wichtige Regeln für den Verfrachter:

❶ Entlaste die Deutsche Reichsbahn von allen entbehrlichen Transporten! Verfrachte mehr als bisher auf dem Wasserweg!

❷ Bestelle Güterwagen rechtzeitig und nur dann, wenn die Gütermenge den Wagenraum restlos ausfüllt. Es ist heute verantwortungslos, mehr Wagen zu bestellen, als unumgänglich nötig sind!

❸ Fülle Frachtbriefe und die sonstigen Begleitpapiere sorgfältig und vollständig aus — übergib sie sogleich nach beendeter Beladung dem Annahmebeamten! So werden Verzögerungen und Irrläufe verhindert!

❹ Gib den Bestimmungsbahnhof im Frachtbrief tarifmäßig richtig an — bezeichne im Frachtbrief auch gleich etwa gewünschte besondere Entladestellen!

❺ Benutze alle nur erdenklichen Hilfsmittel zur vollkommenen Ausnutzung des Wagenraumes! Oft helfen Einbauten. Bei offenen Wagen erhöht das Aufborden der Wagenwände das Fassungsvermögen für leichte Güter.

❻ Belade Reichsbahngüterwagen im Inlandsverkehr bis zu 2000 kg über die angeschriebene Tragfähigkeit hinaus, im Verkehr mit den besetzten Gebieten und einigen Nachbarstaaten (Auskunft erteilen die Güterabfertigungen) bis 1000 kg über die Tragfähigkeit, belgische und französische Wagen im Inlandsverkehr mit 1000 kg über die Tragfähigkeit!

❼ Verhüte Wagenschäden durch Innehalten der Lademaße und ordnungsgemäße, betriebssichere Verladung! Kein Güterwagen darf heute durch vermeidbare Ausbesserungsarbeiten dem Verkehr entzogen werden!

❽ Bereite alle Ladearbeiten so vor, daß mit der Be- und Entladung s o f o r t nach Bereitstellung der Güterwagen begonnen werden kann. Setze a l l e Hilfskräfte und a l l e technischen Hilfsmittel hierfür ein!

❾ Während der Ladearbeiten darf es heute keine Pause geben. Ladearbeiten dürfen Tag und Nacht, wochentags, sonn- und feiertags nicht ruhen, solange noch ein Wagen zu be- oder entladen ist. Überschreitung von Ladefristen darf es nicht mehr geben! Auf jede Stunde kommt es an!

❿ Der Güterwagen ist kein Lagerraum! Güterwagen müssen rollen! Tu als Verfrachter alles, um Wagenstillstand zu vermeiden! Verzögerte Entladung hat Zwangsentladung, Zwangszufuhr, unter Umständen Strafen zur Folge!

Die Front erwartet, daß die Heimat ihr den notwendigen Nachschub liefert. Hierzu wird jeder Güterwagen gebraucht.

Tu' auch Du Deine Pflicht! Sorge für beste Ausnutzung der Güterwagen und vermeide jeden unnötigen Wagenstillstand!

GEBR. FEYL ⬤ BERLIN SW

"Every freight car is used": DR placard from 1942.

8

One minute faster

"Two years ago, in March 1940, the coal agreement between Germany and Italy was signed. When the agreement was made, a British journalist calculated that a coal train would have to cross the border to Italy every twenty minutes. But the calculation was not quite right: Every 19 minutes would have been the correct and precise number."

Vereinssetzung, March 1942

Mussolini's fall at the end of 1943 and the surrender required a transfer of the Italian trains still in the *Wehrmacht's* territory. In Verona the Italian WVD was established; its management remained with the Italian State Railways (FS). And the earlier general representation of the *Reichsbahn* in Rome was renamed the "Railroad Commander of the *Reichsbahn*." The WVD was formed similarly to a field railroad command and directed its own personnel; only the purely military service posts were occupied by field-gray command officers.

Italy's front change and the withdrawal of the German troops meant a further burden for the entire transport and traffic system. For these problems, the General of Transport in Italy was assigned to the army group. Subordinate to him was an outside office in Florence, which included the transport offices in Rome, Ancona, and finally Genoa, Milan, and Turin as well. The front areas to Monte Cassino, Nettuno on the Mediterranean, and Pescara on the Adriatic were subordinate to the office in Florence. It oversaw and operated a network of some 4500 km of rail lines. But on account of Allied air raids, usually only half of them could be kept open for traffic. Bridges, tunnels, depots, open stretches, and electric power lines were often destroyed. The electric connections were especially important for rail traffic, since the steep lines in the mountains with their many long tunnels could not be handled by steam locomotives.

When the Allies slowly marched northward up the boot of Italy in the winter of 1943-44, the German resistance began to stiffen, and the supply needs of the German *Wehrmacht* for carrying out their operations rose, according to estimates, to 300 tons a day.

All the air raids concentrated on breaking the rail network and preventing its rebuilding. They compelled the German army to turn to road transport and coastal shipping, which was done at the cost of German fuel reserves. Bridges, tunnels, railroad operational works, and freight depots were now the most important targets of a great Allied air offensive. The traffic network, with its rolling trains, became a rewarding objective for the fighter-bombers.

Trains for *Wehrmacht* transport were armed with light Flak guns for defense against low-flying planes. On electrified tracks, though, the guns could not be used without disturbing the power lines. For this reason, the design of an optical-electric fire-control device was considered, which would prevent firing as soon as parts of the overhead wires came into the line of fire, but it remained only a wish.

The Reich Research Council had the idea of fighting off low-flying attacks on locomotives by splinter fire. The guns were to be attached to the locomotives and fitted with an automatic acoustic trigger. The Germans were looking forward to the bad surprise for the low-flyers who sighted a fire-spitting locomotive, but this project also existed only on paper.

Sensitive Groceries

"Often express packages of food that are sent to *Wehrmacht* members at their garrisons cannot be delivered because the recipient has meanwhile been called to front service. If such parcels, even in they do not exceed the weight of 5 kg, can be sent right back to the sender, it is to be feared that in many cases the sensitive groceries will spoil during the return trip. Such foods are sent on, in agreement with the applicable food office, when no other instructions are given by the sender. But there is also the possibility of sending undeliverable foods to a *Wehrmacht* hospital at no cost, if the sender has so stated his agreement on the express tag. The *Reichsbahn* asks that as extensive use of this option as possible be made."

DNB, April 1943

The protection of the trains in the occupied eastern areas was the job of the *Wehrmacht*, and was organized by the *Wehrmacht* transport offices. It was limited essentially to important depots and large bridgebuilding works. Thus, partisan attacks were generally directed at the open stretches of rail lines. To guard these lines and important objects, German home guard units, soldiers from allied countries, and local helpers (Hiwis) were used. But this protection was far from sufficient. The helper troops were extremely unreliable. On August 17, 1943, local helpers—some 600 men—went over, almost as a group, to the partisans, taking all their weapons.

South of Minsk, on the Minsk-Ossipowici-Gomel line, isolated rail sentry posts were attacked by partisans in broad daylight.

They had to deliver railroad-building tools such as spike crowbars, screwdrivers, and the like, with which the partisans could rip up the tracks somewhere. The line protection, spread too thin and much too weak, was often surrounded at depots and *Wehrmacht* support points, and put down easily during the activities of partisan mine-laying and explosive units.

Countermeasures to eliminate these disturbances generally proved to be makeshift solutions. For example, to secure the short but important Shlobin-Gomel rail line, which was exposed to frequent partisan attacks, arriving transports were unloaded on the line, and soldiers—a man every five meters—were positioned to protect them. Despite that, further explosions took place!

To make at least one line usable again, not only passing lines but also rails of the second main line were removed and installed in the line that could be repaired most quickly. Damaged cars were tipped off the line. Above all, troop and ammunition trains were sent on longer trips on lines where acts of sabotage had not yet or only rarely taken place. In longer delays, the service often ran on only one track. If both tracks were blocked, the trains were gathered at the depots and sent through the damaged place as soon as one line was usable again. For line examinations made by officers of the transport service or railroad engineers, the slow-flying "Fieseler Stork" of the *Luftwaffe* proved useful.

The material losses, especially of ties, rails, locomotives, and cars, hit the DRB hard. An attack with magnetic mines on a depot between Minsk and Gomel in July 1943 destroyed a fuel train, two ammunition trains, and a train carrying the most modern German tanks of the "Tiger" type. The loss of locomotives was especially catastrophic. In September 1943, 649 locomotives were damaged in the entire GVD East, 357 of them so badly that they had to be sent to Germany to be repaired.

Whenever the general traffic on the line let up, removal trains with crane cars went out to lift the derailed but still-intact cars back onto the rails. One of the two especially strong 90-ton cranes of the German *Reichsbahn* was sent to the Minsk district. Insufficiently protected, it became a victim of an explosive attack.

Great Need for Reading Matter and Wall Decorations
"Among the fellow workers of the German *Reichsbahn* in the occupied territories, there is a great need for reading matter, pictures and wall decorations for their service, living and communal rooms. The wall bookcases and pictures made by the *Reichsbahn* could only partly satisfy the need. The workers at the small offices in particular, and at the positions that were far from the supplying central offices, could be supplied only slightly to date. These particular places need special supplying.

The Reich Traffic Minister thus calls on our fellow workers to help improve the living and working conditions for our comrades in the East by donating books and pictures. The collecting will be handled by the *Reichsbahn* Comradeship Works."

NSBZ-Voraus, 3-4 1943

Lonely depots and signals had meanwhile been protected by barriers, palisades, and defense installations. Even the smaller stream culverts were rebuilt into heavily armed forts. On lines that ran through wooded areas, German engineers cut down trees, sometimes up to 200 meters from the tracks. Whoever entered these areas, identified as prohibited zones, had to expect to be fired on immediately. The help trains with the construction troops now had military escorts, commands of 15 to 30 men in bulletproof vehicles—also called "*Berta-Wagons*." When possible, several trains traveled together at a speed of 20 kph to prevent the partisans from laying new mines in the interim. By day, individual trains moved at a speed of 40 kph, at night only 25 kph. On not too heavily used lines the traffic was generally stopped at night. The trains then had to stay until dawn at the last depot they reached before nightfall. The first train could not go faster than 25 kph, after the line had been checked for mines by either *Wehrmacht* patrols or trained railroad men. But the partisans, who lurked in their hiding places along the tracks by the thousands, then changed their tactics and made their attacks in daylight more and more often. So that at least the locomotive would not be damaged when mines exploded, two open freight cars were coupled in front. Even in daylight, no train could run without a protective car in front nor exceed 40 kph.

And transport trains had to hitch the cars occupied by people on the rear. Furlough and passenger trains were also given another protective car behind the locomotive.

"*The* Ostbahn *is one of the lifelines of German victory,*" said General Governor Frank on May 25, 1943. In his diary, Frank entered a report from the leader of the main railroad department of the General Government, Gerteis, which sums up the transport situation as follows:

"The number of explosions, attacks on stations and railroad facilities is rising steadily from February to May of this year. At this time we reckon on an average of 10 or 11 attacks per day. Many lines can be traveled by day only with an escort, for example, the Luckow-Lublin line. Another line, the Zavada-Rava-Ruskaine, could only be used by the day or hour and is otherwise out of use."

The building service of the General Government, which had recruited young Poles forcibly even in the Krakow district, made them available to the *Ostbahn* for urgent work on the tracks, similarly to the Organisation Todt or the Reich Work Service (RAD) in Germany.

The locksmith *Alyosha Nikolaievich Prokopyenke*, then 19 years old and working at the repair shop in Poltava, became a partisan. He reported:

"Since we had to know the approximate schedule for the blowing up of an important rail line, and it was not always possible to find out from our associates in the city, we had to find ways to help ourselves. Besides, we had always been ordered to observe the trains that went by, which was not so easy. If one of us was caught in the so-called 'forbidden zone,' we could consider him lucky if he were shot at once—it could also happen that he would be given a painful questioning first. So we always sought a suitable hiding place as an observation post. The safest was an especially thick tree stump with roots, that could be hollowed out carefully from below, and into which we cut small slits all around. Then we dragged it to our observation post during the night and dug a big round hole, in which we placed a small bench. Then the observer, with his food bag full of bread, bacon, and several bottles of water, squeezed in, and the hollowed-out tree stump was placed over him. Thus, he could make his observations unseen for several days.

After we learned in this way when the trains came through, precise plans for laying mines could be made.

Before we sent out the minelayer, the color and type of soil at the site had to be known; a bag of soil of the same color, equally damp or dry, was found—plus a bottle of water, and if necessary, a hoe. We made the spade we used to bury the mine out of wood, so it was more quiet. The minelayer, after he had buried the mine, had to arrange the ground just as it was before, spread out the soil he had brought along, smooth it or hoe it, and water it to blend in with the ground around it.

To be sure, the laying of mines got to be more and more problematic in time. The soil along the tracks was either rolled flat or hoed in patterns by the Germans. Besides, spotlights were set up, and so the comrades of the explosive unit could only roll along the rails, they could not [robben] at all. It is clear that they thus left behind undeniably wide tracks, which they had to remove without a trace. Just approaching the tracks and leaving the place without any trace was, aside from the mine-laying itself, a special task that demanded the last from the men.

And then the Germans realized that our mines, which could not be found with their mine-seeking devices because of their wooden packing boxes, contained TNT. They trained their dogs to recognize the smell of TNT and at first were very successful. But we soon had a countermeasure: the openings of the mines were stuffed with powdered Machorka tobacco or snuff. But the smell of Machorka was often not sufficient, and finally we found the right solution: in ever-changing distances from the mine we buried several tiny pieces of TNT. That helped. The dogs were completely confused—they sniffed and barked like mad, ran back and forth, dug up the ground—and found nothing.

When we blew up railroad lines, we always had to be sure that the chosen place was as far as possible from the nearest depot or German garrison. In the first light of morning, we went to our exit point on the railroad line.

First we cut the telephone and telegraph lines. Some of the group, the best shots, hid in the bushes opposite the point where the middle of the derailed train would probably lie—some 100 to 150 paces away from the mine. Other comrades lurked on both sides of the roadbed opposite the mined place with machine guns, so that they could take the whole area under fire. Two small groups—some 10 to 15 comrades—went half a kilometer forward and back, where they prepared traps that would stop the Germans who were called to help. Then we had to wait patiently. The worst problem at such times was the gnats that got into our noses, mouths, and eyes. We couldn't stand it for a minute. Even tar, the old established material that we had rubbed on our faces and hands, no longer helped. The gnats seemed to have gotten used to it over time. Meanwhile, I had to sneak up to the roadbed with my two mine-layers, to the nearest joint in the rails, and place the mine under it. Often I found that our watchman reported, just at the moment when we wanted to start, that German track walkers were coming. Then we slipped quickly back into the bushes and let them go past us, so they wouldn't notice our work.

Naturally, when the mine was already laid, there was usually nothing else for us to do but quickly liquidate the track-walker troop and, without waiting for the train, blow up the tracks and disappear.

When we had gained more experience, we then built very special mines that not only reacted to the pressure of the locomotive or cars, but also had a so-called pull igniter that exploded when they tried to remove it. A mine with one of them attached could not be removed, even by the devil."

The research department of the *Reichsbahn* test center in Munich even developed an automatic alarm for track surveillance. Trip wires were to be pulled along the railroad tracks. They were linked with electric bells and had easily released break couplings. When the wire was broken, the alarm device was turned on, and one knew at once on which line the partisans were to be looked for. But even before the wires were moved the partisans got wind of them. On the next morning the alarm devices had disappeared, and instead of the tracks, they secured the partisans' hiding places.

Another creation of the research department was the "*Guewa*" track surveillance apparatus. This was an electric measuring apparatus that was built into block signals and told by electric pulses whether the track in the area of the signal was in order. If explosions took place, or if just the attachments were unscrewed, the signal device showed it immediaely, and the endangered trains could be stopped in time.

To make the planted mines explode before they were set off by a train, the special "*Rema*" minesweeping vehicle was developed. The driverless motor car was started by a driver at the station of departure; he jumped off at the right time and rode on the locomotive of the following train. If the stretch of track was free of mines, the vehicle was stopped automatically at the next station by a special stopping device. The "Rema" usually rolled along several hundred meters ahead of the protected train. Its design was that of a simple motorized car that pushed a two-ton ignition car ahead of itself on a long rod.

The ignition car was built of pieces of scrap, and caterpillar treads were welded onto its tires to make strong swings during the trip, so as to detonate the mines with vibration fuses. The simple contact mines were set off by the ignition car itself, which despite its low weight had the effect on the track, with the treads welded onto it, of a locomotive with 20-ton axle pressure. The stick mines were exploded by a hoop. For use against the mines that the partisans ignited by remote control, an apparatus had been developed that tore off the lead wires or cords at the right time. If a mine exploded, then "Rema" released a brake mechanism that stopped it before the bomb crater and showed the oncoming train the dangerous place by means of blinking lights. But soon the partisans built their mines differently, so that they were only set off by the ignition and motor cars. The "Rema" now rolled over the mine, and only the locomotive following two or three minutes later set off the contact. Attempts were made with an added device to master this new problem. A high-frequency transmitter was mounted in the motor car and in contact with the ignition car via a dipolar antenna. Over the antenna an electromagnetic field closed, eliciting a power surge despite the still-open power circle of the mine. It would have been almost impossible for the enemy to find a countermeasure. But this perfect setup never was put into use. On May 6, 1944—five years after the war began—just as the German Army was about to finish its withdrawal from the Soviet Union, the German General Staff gave out training instructions that included methods of fighting the partisans. Not just a few months later, when the troops could have made use of the guidelines, the Wehrmacht was no longer fighting on Soviet soil.

The goal of the partisan action to cripple all the railroads was not achieved thanks to the countermeasures, even though it was not uncommon for rail lines to be closed for days or even weeks. But the partisans did hinder the Wehrmacht and economic traffic considerably, and cause general insecurity in the backlines. Through delays in troop movement and difficult front supplying, the railroad at times lost the character of a reliable help to waging war.

A brief meeting at the depot in Tschernowitz: two nurses of the Hungarian Red Cross in a passenger car of the Hungarian railroad (MAV), late autumn 1942.

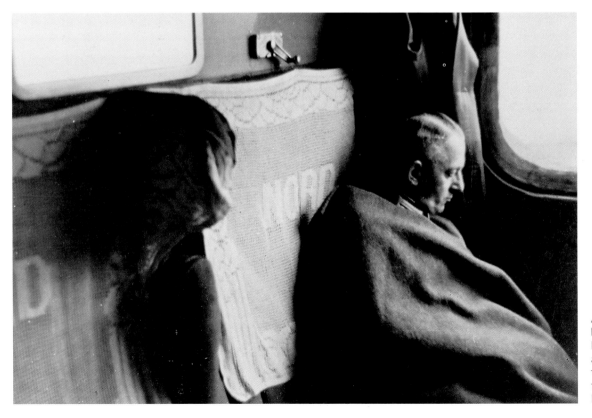

A nap during a trip between Brussels and Paris, December 1942: in a second-class express train compartment of the former northern railroad line of France.

The last check at the station: a member of the furlough supervision command does his duty. Roslavl, November 1942.

Rostock, December 1942: a short coffee break on the way to the front.

Autumn 1942: an ammunition train blown up by partisans near Smolensk.

Sicherung der Wasserdurchlassstelle

Recommended by the OKH: model of a culvert-securing site on an eastern line.

Malin, west of Kiev, December 1942: a freight locomotive of Series 55^{25} with frost protection around the pump and frontal camouflage is under steam.

Eastern front, winter 1942-43: a lone sentry watches over a *Wehrmacht* transport.

April 1943; a woman conductor puts up the signal plates.

April 1943; ticket check.

A barbershop under the open sky; beside it a Polish locomotive of Ty 23 type near Radom, March 1943.

Spring 1943: DR locomotives of Series 93^5 with white blackout paint on the water tanks and buffers. In the background is a German railroad workshop.

Korosten, May 1943: farewell to the comrades. The three-axle compartment car is in use by the DR-East.

Warsaw Ghetto, March 1943: on the way to the extermination camp.

Near the Kiev depot, May 1943: a soldier and two farm women quickly make a deal.

July 5, 1943, Bachtmatsch: Otto—that's what the soldiers called fuel—is here! At the right time, on the eve of Operation "Citadel," the German attack in the Kursk Bend. The tank car shows the newly introduced abbreviation "DR."

A short stop in Minsk, July 1943: improvised performance before a very skeptical public.

Dienstanweisung

für die

Handhabung des Betriebsdienstes auf den belgischen und französischen Eisenbahnen nach Einführung des

Notfahrplanes

═══ „D A Not" ═══

Nur für den Dienstgebrauch

Diese « D A Not » tritt auf besondere Anordung der WVD Brüssel bzw Paris in Kraft

Druck : WVD-Brüssel

Reichsverkehrsdirektion Kiew

Verkehrsarchiv
beim Verkehrsmuseum Nürnberg

Vorläufige Bestimmungen

für das

Fahren auf Sicht

Gültig vom 1. Februar 1943 an

Deutsche Reichsbahn

Verkehrsarchiv
beim Verkehrsmuseum Nürnberg

Anleitung

zur

Verständigung mit dem russischen Personal

Betriebsdienst

(Sprachanleitung)

Herausgegeben
im Auftrage des Reichsverkehrsministeriums, Zweigstelle Osten, von der Reichsbahndirektion Breslau

A 6 H 84 8 c 70 in 7 d Breslau XI 42 17 000 B.0049

Wehrmacht-Frachtbrief
(Frachtberechnung und Abrechnung nachträglich zu den vereinbarten Sätzen)

Deutsche Wehrmacht

August 1943, Cherbourg: liverwurst for the builders of the "Atlantic Wall." Reich Work Service men unload a DR freight car from the Hannover district.

From Shisdra to Munich main depot, June 23, 1943: a DR label pasted onto *Wehrmacht* goods.

Gironde, June 1943: a group of RAD men with their baggage. At left is a four-axle passenger car of the French railways.

Farewell: two information helpers at left a captured dining car of the ISG in La Rochelle, May 1943.

9

Children Travel to Switzerland

"Invited by the administration of the Swiss Federal Railroad, 100 children of German railroaders can be sent for a seven-week stay in Switzerland. The children spend the first four weeks of their Swiss visit in Weissenburg, in the idyllic Simme Valley, not far from Spiez. They spend the other three weeks in picturesque Beatenberg on the north shore of Thun Lake, 1200 meters high, with a view of the mighty Alpine landscape on the other side, especially the Bluemis-Alp."

DNB, July 1943

In Germany itself, railroad operations were still satisfactory until the summer of 1943, although bomber raids increased more and more. In the spring of 1944, the destruction of transport routes took on the foremost place in Allied air-war strategy: on one hand, to prepare for the invasion, and on the other, to cripple German war production. Yet it was not so much the fighter-bomber attacks as the carpet bombing of railroad depots and intersections that had a negative effect.

Travel, to be sure, became more and more risky, but people adjusted to it. When the alarm sirens sounded, the railroad depots hoisted a yellow warning flag. And the trains tried to get out of the depot areas as quickly as possible. Every locomotive driver had to know the terrain along the rail lines, so as to seek shelter in woodlands or tunnels. Remarkably, though, there were no official regulations for passengers to follow in such cases. The travelers, taught by experience, left the trains and hid themselves in patches of woods along the tracks or in air raid ditches beside the lines. If the tracks were damaged, they often had to walk to the nearest depot, or to replacement trains, with all their belongings. At the great depots, the passengers not only streamed into the safe bomb shelters from the platforms when the alarm sounded, but also from the nearby streets. The regular sale of tickets often could not be carried out for days after air raids. Thus, the Red Cross was on the scene quickly with field kitchens and distributed hot food to the travelers.

In 1943 the crowding of passenger trains increased more and more because the schedules were shortened. In addition, millions of people left the cities that were threatened by bomb attacks; in

Hamburg alone they numbered 602,000 people. Despite the air raids on numerous important rail junctions, such as Cologne, Berlin, Hamburg, Hanover, Hamm, Kassel, or Mannheim-Ludwigshafen, the DRB was always able, until April 1945, to restore passenger service to some extent. And the population did not let danger and tension deter them from traveling.

To deal with the damage to rail lines, "elastic operation" became the policy. The local offices were given a free hand to do what was most sensible and necessary in their own districts, depending on the state of things. In hardest-hit Hamm, 9000 OT workers worked constantly to repair damage. But as of mid-1944, since construction workers were called from the Atlantic Wall, the OT work columns had enough workers available.

In the many branch offices of the *Reichsbahn*, especially in operations, the number of employed German women reached 182,000 from 1943 to 1945.

Despite all efforts, Allied air raids threatened to shake the firm organization of the *Reichsbahn*. Soon more than 2000 trains blocked the transit lines, so that even "Blitz shipments" with the highest level of urgency could no longer reach their destinations on time. On May 30, 1944, about a week before the invasion in Normandy, the German railroad network had been hit so hard that even a long pause in air raids by the Allies could scarcely eliminate the transit problems.

Transport was now only possible from depot to depot, damage to damage. Ganzenmueller and Speer used local transit employees to pilot freight trains through the wasteland of tracks.

Camouflage

"The camouflage of industrial, transport and service facilities important to the war has a special significance in air war. Their job consists of keeping such sites as safe as possible from enemy action from the air. This is done either through direct disguising of the sites to be protected, such as railroad operations centers, power plants, etc., or disguising especially characteristic facilities—track lines, rivers, canals, roads, etc.—that, because of their particular situation or formation in the areas of the sites to be protected, can serve as approach and orientation points to enemy aviators."

Reichsbahn, 11-12 1943

Alarm

Fliegerangriffe bedrohen vor allem **größere Bahnhöfe.**

Reisende, Ihr werdet **rechtzeitig** gewarnt! Wahrt Ruhe und Besonnenheit! Befolgt die Anordnungen der Beamten!

Verlaßt die Bahnhöfe auf kürzestem Wege und sucht den nächsten **Sammelschutzraum** auf! Züge nur auf Weisung verlassen!

Jeder Lichtschein zeigt dem Flieger sein Ziel. **Wahrt Lichtdisziplin!** Keine Taschenlampen!

"…practice quiet and prudence!" Autumn 1943.

Left: construction of a Series 52 war locomotive in February 1943. The machines still have bar frames. Right: riveting the bolts on a boiler.

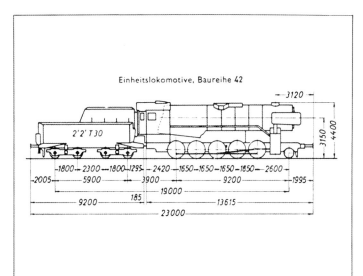

Einheitslokomotive, Baureihe 42

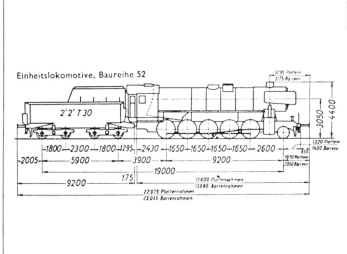

Einheitslokomotive, Baureihe 52

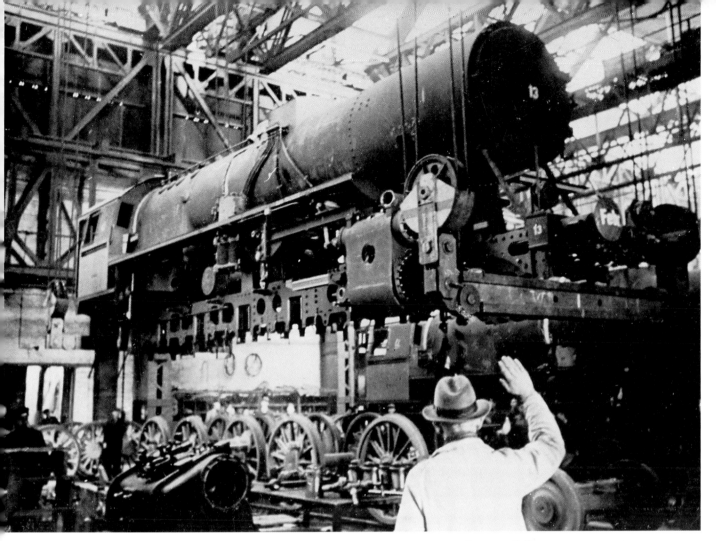

Mounting boilers on axles of 40 locomotives that Borsig built in February 1943.

July 7, 1943: the Seddin freight yards near Berlin. Fifty-one Series 52 war locomotives, the highest daily production achieved by all German locomotive factories to date, set out on their way.

Before the great parade of war locomotives at Seddin, near Berlin, they pose for the press and newsreels, July 7, 1943. At left are locomotives with Viennese rigid-frame tenders and extended frost protection.

Berlin, autumn 1943: a heavy flak battery protect important railway facilities.

October 1943: the assembly hall of the Berliner Maschinenbau AG, formerly L. Schwartzkopff. The Series 52 war locomotives are in the final stages of assembly; in the background, WR 360 C 14 three-axle *Wehrmacht* Diesel locomotives are being built.

Breslau, October 1943: passenger cars have been rebuilt as a DR hospital train. Beside it is a Red Cross vehicle of the 168th Infantry Division.

Left: Summer 1943. A makeshift armored train equipped with captured Russian tanks serves to protect the rail line between Vinniza and Berdichev.

Lower left: Orsha, early September 1943: the cab of a DR-East freight locomotive, Series 57[10], from Smolensk-East.

Right: Summer 1943, on the line between Siedice and Brest-Litovsk a Polish Ty 23 locomotive from the Siedice works is being tapped.

Landshut, September 1943: a 15-ton crane goes on a trip. At left is a four-axle stakeside car, at right a low-side car from the Erfurt district.

Lower left: Kovel, September 1943: one of thousands of nameless blue railroaders on duty near the front.

Right: morning wash-up in the yards at Budweis, September 1943. The water comes from a Wuppertal type water tank car from the Schwerte works.

The railroad line between Aix-en-Provence and Marseille, summer 1943: the baggage train of a German division on the way to Italy.

Italy 1943: a German armored division rides through the Apennines.

10

The Soviet offensives were aimed particularly at transit junctions. And the battle for Stalingrad, one of the most important transit junctions, was of decisive importance to the Red Army. Here two of the most important rail lines met: the Orel—Voronesh—Povarino line from the north and the Rostov—Kostelnikovo line from the south.

The collapse of the Don front, the German defeat on the peninsula of Kuban, and the final loss of Kharkov and Byelgorod show the soviet strategy of winning back the Kharkov—Poltava—Rostov and Sumy-Byelgorod—Kursk main lines. The great winter offensive of the Soviets, that began on November 22, 1942, set practically insoluble tasks for the German *Reichsbahn*. The front moved back from the Volga and Terek to the Don and Mius. Thus, 450,000 square kilometers of land, with the entire network of Field Railroad Command 3, plus the Reich Transit Direction in Rostov, were lost. The Red air fleet concentrated its attacks on the backline supply links of the Germans, and the Soviet armies pushed forward into the backlands, broke the rail lines, and thus made supplying and evacuating the front impossible. Thus, the railroad junctions such as Kursk, Lgov, Belgorod, Isyum, Vyasma, and Rshev were regained by the Soviets.

The German retreat in the East began on July 5, 1943. On this day attempts were made on the Kursk Bend front, in the so-called Operation "*Citadel*," to change the fortunes of war through the use of modern weapons, but the plan failed. On July 12, 1943, the Soviets attacked Orel. Ten days later, on 2 July, the front that curved forward had to be given up. The DRB was able to dismantle railroad workshops and other facilities and move them westward. The simultaneous mass explosions of rail lines by partisans, plus heavy air attacks on the main lines and junction depots, introduce the great withdrawal movement, which began in the southern and central sectors of the eastern front early in August 1943.

The time of the German defeats on the eastern front caused one of the transport system's greatest problems. On the one had, as few men and materials as possible should fall into enemy hands; on the other, the most important transit links had to be made unusable for the advancing Red Army.

Often the blow-up order—for reasons of secrecy or recognition of the situation—was delayed so long that there was finally not enough time for the destruction. In the withdrawal from the front at the end of 1943, the *Wehrmacht* requested that new lines be built as cross-connections. But the railroad engineers were so busy with destruction tasks that they had no time to repair the backland lines that had been blown up by partisans.

The evacuation of the Kiev rail junction, though, was introduced at the right time, so that by November 5, 1943, 24,911 cars with valuable freight, and all the facilities and bridges, could be destroyed completely.

The Germans usually cut rail attachments as they withdrew, so that the Soviet engineers had to install new ones before converting to broad gauge.

It can be seen, though, that they were nevertheless in a situation to restore the destroyed lines very quickly—often with the help of German prisoners of war. On November 6, 1943, the conquered railroad junction at Kiev was already in use again, and on 24 November the first trains crossed the Dniepr at Kiev. The withdrawal after the battles of Vyasma and Rshev, code name "Buffalo Movement," could be handled by "careful" transport preparations for both personnel and materials, almost without losses. The front length of 754 km was shortened to 386 km; the furthest withdrawal measured 160 km in 2 days; 24,000 square kilometers of land were thus given up.

The difficulties of withdrawal showed clearly in the extraordinary demands on the available locomotives for countless switchings, strong increases of troop transports and supply trains until right at the war zone, and also through constant lack of power. One example of that is the withdrawal from Kharkov, which went on non-stop day and night. The magazine, workshops, camps, and storage places at the edge of the city had more than 200 rail junctions in all. But both empty trains and returning transports had to be directed through the depots that were stuffed full of trains whose destinations were already in Soviet hands. Hundreds of cars with coal, hay, straw, or barrack components had to be unloaded first to make room for more important goods.

With these hindrances, transporting army materials could scarcely be considered. There were 8000 cars in Kharkov, 2000 more than at the beginning of the withdrawal. The switching work reached an extent that could no longer be mastered.

In the entire Kharkov area, army engineers prepared explosive charges, so that the remaining freight of the *Wehrmacht* would not fall into the enemy's hands and even increase his fighting power.

In the first week of February, a surprising Soviet advance set the city in an uproar. An air-landed troop had been landed near Balakleya, between Isyum and Kharkov, had blown up the rail line there, captured a few depot crews and, in the exuberance of success, even telephoned the main railroad direction in Kharkov.

On February 16, 1943, the II. SS Armored Corps (SS *Obergruppenfuehrer* Hauser) gave up Kharkov contrary to Hitler's orders. What was lost there is unimaginable. There were vast amounts of food, pleasure and medicinal goods, implements, weapons, ammunition, clothing, motors—things that the typical citizen of the Reich could not imagine even being present there. Until the last moment, irrational pursers hung onto everything, instead of giving it to soldiers passing through. In the end, only a fraction of it could be burned or blown up; the rest fell into enemy hands.

The collapse of Army Group Center toward the end of June 1944 endangered the German transport system considerably, especially through the loss of useful unloading facilities near the front. Even worse, the surrendered transport lines and facilities could not be destroyed at the right time, and the stores, workshops, and parks could not be emptied. The loss of locomotives in the East in November 1943 alone added up to 673 damaged units, 333 of them badly. Opposed to this, only 400 to 500 new locomotives could be built per month.

Chief Inspector *Kurt Walther,* one of the blue railroad men, experienced the withdrawal:

"On June 2, 1944, the third anniversary of the advance into the USSR, the Red Armies went on the offensive, and more quickly than anyone had ever feared, broke through between Orsha and Borissov. The Soviet shock-troop wedges pushed forward over the Beresina into the district of the blue administration and rolled over the railroad men, who were often the last to hold fast and vacated on command 'without regard for losses.'"

In endless chains of trains, the withdrawal traffic flowed from the directions of Minsk and Sluzk. The troop transport and supply traffic in both directions poured into the Baranowitz depots, which were still suffering from the effects of air raids, and after changing locomotives as quickly as possible, they went out again. There was no limited service time any more.

And while they had to begin to evacuate Baranowitz itself, more and more freight from Germany rolled in. The transport officers in the hinterlands operated according to a regular schedule. They were either not yet informed of the changed situation, or they did not dare to stop the shipping of freight without orders from above.

The population, enveloped in clouds of smoke and dust, made the best of it. The line to Lida was choked. To relieve it, a number of trains were called back and sent via Volkovysk. The depot at Yegiornika, shortly before Volkovysk, was heavily overrun by fighter planes on the afternoon of 5 July. Along with the difficulties resulting from the air raid on Yegiornika, fire attacks were made near Slonim at night, so that in the morning thirteen "Richard trains" were stuck between Polonka and Slonim. There the auxiliary train leadership proved itself. It was able not only to move the trains on through multiple quick changes from homeland rails to front rails, but at the same time to bring needed trains through to Bara. On the Brest line in Kosov, Ivacewicze, Domanovo, and especially in Lesna, troop and supply trains of all kinds were assembled.

The next day, the evacuation of Slonim was also in full swing, while at the same time heavy traffic from Volkovysk was handled. Polonka had to be given up and the depot blown up. Albertin was now the operations center. Part of the train administration stayed in Slonim, and the command train of the operations office went to Zelva, the border of the Minsk and Koenigsberg administrations. One air raid followed another. Troops were unloaded and wounded men loaded in. The personnel of the train leadership handled switchng.

On 9 July Albertin was given up. The new operations base was Slonim itself. While battle noise could be heard and two air raids had to be survived, the loading of damaged tanks took place, and the Vimy supply store was emptied.

After a brief improvement of the tactical situation, the enemy's threats to the depot and rail line grew so strong that the railroaders fled from Slonim around 11:00.

And what had begun with Stalingrad a year and a half ago went on and on, from depot to depot. The native railroad crews fled everywhere, and trains had to run without escorts, without [Zugschluss], and with too many axles. None of the service instructions could be considered any more. Troop and ammunition trains ran, empty material was transported to the battle line, and groups of evacuation trains were run out of burning depots until the moment when the engineers set off the prepared charges. Cars were switched on bombed tracks, over broken rails and patched switches. In the main depots, empty trains to be loaded with wounded men and damaged tanks were held until the last minute. A main hindrance to operations in the main depots was the explosive trains. On 22 July the main depot in Bialystok became the operational headquarters in the direction of Grodno. On the station one could read in huge letters: "Wheels must roll for victory. The rail wolf tore the last stretch of track from Bialsk to Bialystok to bits."

The Soviet summer offensive that began on June 22, 1944, in the course of which the German Army Group Center collapsed, caused by far the greatest vehicle losses in the eastern campaign.

In Orel, the Donetz Basin, Kiev, Lemberg, Warsaw, and several other cities it was still possible to carry out operations on schedule and thus save valuable material. Often, though, the enemy advance appeared so surprisingly, as in Fastov, Schitomir, Rasdelnaya, Mogilev, Baranovice, Brest-Litovsk, or Lukov, that the railroad men had to leave everything behind and were only able to save their own lives. In Kovel, Vitebsk, Estonia, and Latvia the railroaders were enclosed in a pocket along with the soldiers.

In the Foremost Line
". . . Men of the German *Reichsbahn* from all parts of the Reich, belonging to all ranks and branches were the ones who, in the bad days of the battles around Kovel, showed their heroism side by side with the soldiers of the Army and *Waffen*-SS, of which history will still tell in later times. They were not soldiers or field railroaders in field-gray coats, but men of the blue railroad army who became front-line soldiers in the chaos of retreat movements in

the East. . . Several hundred railroaders found themselves in this pocket, and only about 5% of them had formerly had military training . . . They went into infantry action in the foremost lines on the front, . . . stood guard day and night knee-deep in icy water, beat back the furious Soviet attacks at all positions, and fought with such bravery and bitterness that the soldiers . . . expressed their unlimited admiration of them again and again."

Reichsbahn, 23-24 1944

The withdrawal action in the General Government, prepared on time, went off almost according to plan. On the line between Krakow and Lemberg in the summer of 1944, 160 trains a week ran in both directions without overwhelming the capacity of the *Ostbahn*.

Napoleon had shown how it went without trains. At the beginning of his Russian campaign he moved at a very high speed, and his troops covered the road from the Beresina to Moscow in eight weeks, while fighting. For the withdrawal on the same road, under Russian pressure, he needed only five weeks. On the other hand, Hitler's divisions needed two summer campaigns to cover the ground between the Dniestr and Volga, and when they were decisively beaten, covered the same stretch in half the time.

At the end of July 1944, the Red Army stood before Warsaw. The functional ability of the railroad service required that the *Ostbahn* administration stay in the city until the last hour. The administration building, which was apart from the German government and police district in the former Polish Traffic Ministry, was equipped with machine-gun mounts, steel blinds on the windows, and several bunkers. And the personnel who were needed to operate the trains remained at the depots.

On August 1, 1944, at 5:00 PM, an uprising broke out in Warsaw. In heavy fighting around the Danzig Depot, 22 railroad men were killed, including the stationmaster, but connections with the depots on the right side of the Vistula were kept up. The depots east of the Vistula, the Warsaw-Prague Improvement Base, and the Marki Bridge Base were completely emptied. To be able to direct the traffic in the still-held western part of the district, the director's and transport commanders' offices were moved to Koluszki, near Lodz, on 5 August. The uprising lasted 63 days and ended on October 2, 1944, with the surrender of the rebels.

"The fact that moving 350,000 people out of Warsaw to their new locations in a short time succeeded . . . is an outstanding achievement by all German service offices. . . Above all, the placement of railroad cars caused the greatest difficulty, since there was a great shortage of cars because of the military situation in the East and West. Thanks to the cooperation of the *Ostbahn* and the personal initiative of the President, Dr. Wiens, this difficulty was also overcome."

These words of praise from the final report of the Governor of the Warsaw District, SA *Gruppenfuehrer* Dr. Ludwig Fischer, to General Governor Hans Frank about "the uprising in Warsaw in 1944" refer to a very special action by the *Reichsbahn*.

All inhabitants of the Polish capital who survived the uprising were loaded into cattle cars and hauled in a western direction. "All men and women who were able to work"—separated from their families—were, on Himmler's orders, "to be transported to the Reich."

This is probably the only case in the history of the railroad when it was asked to move all the inhabitants of a capital city "to a new location." This task too was fulfilled "in a short time." And in fact, Warsaw was without inhabitants from October 3, 1944, to January 17, 1945. Only explosive commands and a small *Wehrmacht* unit still remained in the city to carry out the Führer's order—"Warsaw shall remain only a geographical concept."

The Dniepr bridge, south of the dam near Saporoshie, August 1943. Two months later the bridge was blown up during the withdrawal.

July 1943, near Pervomaisk: German railroad engineers are building the General Gercke Bridge.

August 28, 1943, near Pervomaisk: the first train over the General Gercke Bridge.

June 1943, Frankfurt on the Oder: this unit was transferred from France to Russia.

A short break: railroaders in the cab of a Series 52 war locomotive, Malkinia 1943.

Summer 1943, between Sarny and Kovel: the wooden railroad bridge over the Styr has been set afire by partisans.

West of Vilna, October 1943: railroad engineers are on their way to new partisan explosion sites.

Summer 1943, at a depot in the Ukraine: waiting for evacuation transport.

Saporoshie, mid-October 1943 transporting wounded men in captured freight cars a few day before the city was captured by Soviet troops.

Vinniza, September 1943: last farewells on the way into the uncertain.

Shepetovka, September 1943: a group of forced laborers must travel to Germany.

Autumn 1943, eastern front, southern sector: a member of a railroad explosion command.

The end on the Dniepr, mid-October 1943: between Krementshug and Dniepropetrovsk the explosive troop tries to slow the Soviet advance.

A dangerous job with a homemade "mine seeker," Autumn 1943, Rovno.

The line between Pinsk and Luninez in former eastern Poland, October 1943: safest route for supplies during the mud period.

Observation and security tower on the threatened tracks near Proskorov autumn 1943.

The 2-cm Flak position protects the important railroad bridge over the Dordogne near Bordeaux, autumn 1943.

Mosyr, autumn 1943: a switch damaged by the partisans.

Between Stolpzy and Minsk, autumn 1943: war locomotive 52 041, pulling a troop transport, just hit a mine.

Farewell at the Leipzig depot, autumn 1943: a hospital train shortly before its departure to the eastern front.

A Series 52 war locomotive pulls express cars on the Stettin-Berlin line, November 1943.

In the cab of a field locomotive, a gray railroader works as the fireman, autumn 1943.

Repairs for a French locomotive shot down by low-flying planes, Cologne-Deutz, autumn 1943.

In German service: locomotives of the SNCF, Type 140 B, of the Western Region, Limoges, autumn 1943.

Autumn 1943, Athens: in a workshop of the former Greek State Railway (SEK).

A French locomotive of the old English type in DR service at Roubaix, autumn 1943.

A special vehicle of Field Railroad command 3 (FEKdo) near Poltava, autumn 1943: a truck of the railroad engineers serves as a rail tractor. Its gauge could be adapted to standard or broad gauge by adjusting the wheels.

Snamenka, west of Kiev, autumn 1943: parting from his son.

A train will come: waiting on a track of Field Railroad Command 3 (FEDko), autumn 1943.

Modena, spring 1944: the "Station Buffet" for the *Wehrmacht*.

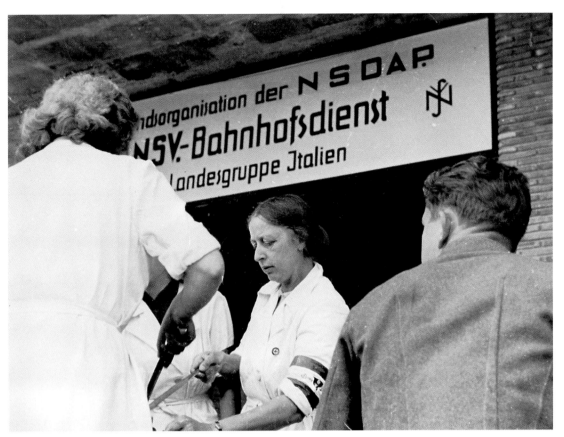

Winter 1943-44: emptying a supply facility near Kharkov.

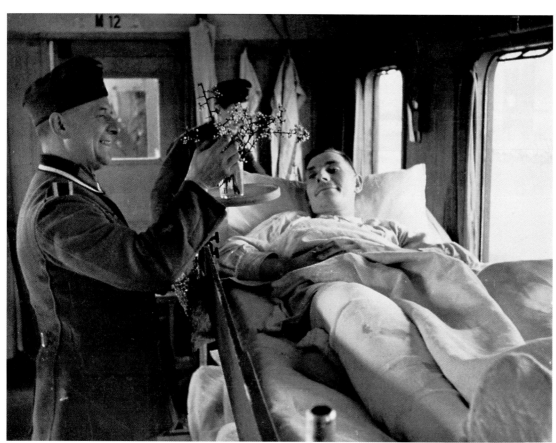

The first herald of spring: a blooming twig in a Bi-passenger car rebuilt as a hospital car, Posen, spring 1944.

Spring 1944, over the Alps: a *Wehrmacht* transport train with a two-axle German stakeside car.

Kirkenes, spring 1944: a car of the Norwegian State Railway (NSB) has been rebuilt as a makeshift armored car.

Spring 1944, in the Minsk area: an armored unit with Assault Gun 40 Type F is transferred by train to a different sector of the front.

A railroad bridge over the Sereth near Bacau, Hungary, spring 1944: this Type 16 passenger locomotive of Austrian origin is hitched on to help pull the train.

An open freight car of the DR, Cottbus autumn 1943.

11

From September 13, 1944, on, Aachen was the first large city on German soil to be fought for. At Hitler's order, Aachen was to be evacuated by its population while the Allies stood at the edge of the city.

The westward movement of the eastern front released a wave of refugees in October 1944 rolling westward on the roads, but mostly on the railroads. The numbers of the trains used to bring families back from the East, and the urgent need of the *Wehrmacht* for supplies, led to considerable disturbances on the lines near the front.

Despite the constant bombing raids on the Reich, three thousand special trains of soldiers, weapons, ammunition, and supplies were sent westward over the Rhine to prepare for the Ardennes offensive in November and December 1944. The preparation of the troops caused one of the most difficult military railroad tasks of World War II. The strictest secrecy was ordered.

The offensive itself suffered from the collapse of the transport system, which was becoming more and more obvious. The required supplies could only be delivered through the uninterrupted highest-quality service of the transport service offices. The oppressive Allied air superiority, though, gradually brought the railroad traffic—in the daytime in particular—to a standstill. The supply service offices could often find the ammunition and fuel trains only with difficulty and unload them only in darkness. Ganzenmueller tried at the end of 1944 to keep the most urgent transports moving through a radical ban on travel. Only a car contingency plan introduced by Ganzenmueller just afterward improved the situation, to the extent that Minister Speer's district authorities could check the urgency of the transports. And while the armament and traffic ministries were still fighting about whether a general ban or car contingency plan was better, the extremely important transit triangle of Hamm-Osnabrueck-Muenster was completely crippled by air raids on December 16, 1944.

On January 13, 1945, sixteen hours after the Soviet winter offensive began, the German 4th Armored Army ceased to exist as a cohesive unit. Within three weeks the Red Army had conquered the rest of Poland, large parts of Germany east of the Oder, and almost all of East Prussia.

The Last Sleeping Cars

"As has been made known, from January 23, 1945, on, the public express and fast train service has been halted. Sleeping cars ran for the last time on the night of 22-23 January. To serve the most urgent war-important service traffic, a few service express trains are in use, but can be used only with a permit from a *Reichsbahn* authority."

DNB, January 22, 1945

At the beginning of 1945 the situation, particularly for the direction regions in the eastern part of the Reich, became more and more difficult. Along with supplies for the front, the refugee transport toward Germany had to be handled.

At the same time as the refugees from East Prussia, about half a million people came west from the Danzig area. Even higher numbers of refugees from the Oppeln district are known. A report by the *Reichsbahn* administration in Posen even spoke of some two million Germans who were transported out of the Warthegau within a few days. There were also 1.7 million Silesians who fled westward, not counting the countless families who set out on foot and used the trains only later. The railroaders of the Katowicz operations office were able on January 27, 1945, to bring the last hospital train from Orzeshe (near Rybmik) to safety under enemy fire.

In January 1945, not only the railroad junctions but also all railroad lines were targets of Allied attacks. On the main lines travel by day was impossible. In the second half of January, frost and snow, as well as the constantly increasing, countless refugee transports from the East, made the situation considerably worse. This traffic situation also had its effect on the armament industry. And the locomotives could be powered only by brown coal. Only in the final stage of the war was a decrease of the achievement of DRB personnel noticeable. The serious destruction of the tracks, the air raids lasting for hours every day, the loss of belongings and goods, often also those of members, were heavy spiritual burdens, and so was poor nourishment.

100,000 Railroaders at the Front

"Another 100,000 railroad men are to be combed out of *Reichsbahn* service for the *Wehrmacht* by order of the *Reichsführer* SS. This is taking place despite a protest from the business-directing Reich Traffic Minister, Dr. Ganzenmueller, who has informed the *Reichsführer* SS that the growing number of accidents in *Reichsbahn* service can be attributed mainly to the preponderance of foreign workers in maintenance work at the locomotive roundhouses and on the lines."
News for the Troops, No. 331, of March 13, 1945 (a handbill from the Psychological Warfare Division, USAAF).

In this chaos, Hitler called Armament Minister Speer to the head of a newly founded transit staff on February 18, 1945. On

20 February Speer was also assigned the division of the entire transport area. A few days after the takeover of the traffic sector by Speer, the U.S. Air Force dealt the death blow to the German transit network with the large-scale Operation "Clarion." Even two million people, mostly unemployed armament workers who were used to repair the damage to the *Reichsbahn* facilities, could not completely overcome the total destruction.

Already in the autumn of 1944 the "Special Measures West" had been ordered. On the lines to the right of the Rhine, west of a determined line, the trains could run almost exclusively at night because of the low-flying air raids; they could travel by day only in foggy weather.

At the beginning of 1945, the Rhine bridges gradually broke down. By the end of February, only two of the nine Rhine bridges in the Cologne area were passable.

On March 18, 1945, Minister Speer appointed to CT Action Group Leader Buerger as General Commissar for the restoration of the *Reichsbahn* facilities. Buerger was given the authority to shut down all building sites so as to free personnel. While the air raids certainly hit the armament hard, they did not fully cripple it, but the destruction of the transport lines had a deadly effect on the life of the *Reichsbahn*.

Führer's Order, March 19, 1945

"The goal is the creation of a transit wasteland in the surrendered area . . . Shortages of explosive materials require inventive use of all possibilities of lasting destruction." Among them are, as details of the order made clear, "bridges of all kinds, tracks, signal boxes, all technical facilities in the freight yards, operational and workshop facilities, but also the dikes and canal locks of our shipping routes. At the same time, all locomotives, passenger and freight cars should be destroyed without a trace."

Since April 1945, Allied air raids knocked out almost the complete internal German railway traffic. 3500 km of tracks, 13,000 switches, 2472 bridges, 30 tunnels, 1500 signals, 110,000 km of telephone lines, 4700 locomotive positions, 9000 locomotives, and 100,000 freight cars fell victim to them. Only 65 percent of the locomotives and 75 percent of the freight cars were still usable.

In mid-April 1945 the organization of the Reich Traffic Ministry, the central administration of the *Reichsbahn*, collapsed. When the contact between the individual services, offices, and administrations finally broke down, that was the end for the DRB.

Northern Italy, Po Valley between Cremona and Mantua, spring 1944: a direct hit on a railroad bridge.

Near Kalinkovici: three blue railroa
men patrol the line in an area plague
by partisans. In the background is a wa
locomotive.

Between Minsk and Borisov, spring 1944: rails damaged by mines; in the background is a makeshift armored train of the railroad engineers.

Spring 1944, near Sluzk: railroad engineers work on rails damaged by partisans.

Air raid alarm! A four-axle Langenschwalbach passenger car as local crew housing.

Boulogne-sur-Mer, March 1944: the end of many supply transports.

Near Luzk, May 1944: as so often, the train that hit a mine was tipped off the track to make the line usable again.

April 1944, Vilna-Duenaburg line: the Soviet pilot paid with his life for his attack on railroad facilities.

May 1944, near Vilkomir: a track security troop on the platform of an old locomotive.

In the vicinity of Kalinkovici, two field-gray railroad men guard a DR Series 56^2 freight locomotive.

Above left: Near Kalinkovici: alarm for the security troop. In the background is a Series 56² freight locomotive.

Above right: The cab of freight locomotive 56 237.

France, spring 1944: resistance members prepare a rail explosion in the vicinity of Bordeaux.

Florence, May 1944: this *Luftwaffe* unit is being transferred southward.

Warsaw, March 1944: a *Luftwaffe* unit stops for food on the way to the front.

Cape Gris Nez, May 1944: a 28 cm railroad gun of the "Bruno" series (1938) on two five-axle turntables.

May 1944, on the line between Kovel and Sarny: forced laborers are laying track.

Between Arras and Lille, summer 1944: a French passenger locomotive after an attack by the Resistance.

Summer 1944, north of Rome:
after a fighter-bomber attack.

Evreux, early June 1944: a typical picture of a French depot north of Paris just before the invasion.

Rouen, May 1944: railroad engineers pick up the pieces of a supply train destroyed by the French Resistance.

June 1944: the Dniepr bridge at Orsha was blown up by partisans.

Normandy, invasion front, June 1944: a German fuel transport destroyed by low-flying Allied planes.

Bordeaux, June 1944: troop-transport protection with a machine gun against low-flying planes. On sidings at both sides are SNCF wine tank cars.

On a blown-up railroad bridge near Gomel.

Paris, late June 1944: two railroaders of the *Wehrmacht* Traffic Administration, a transport organization of the *Reichsbahn*, examine the car cards while on duty in France after the Allied landing in Normandy.

France, July 1944: three members of the WVD (*Wehrmacht* Traffic Administration) at a Paris depot.

Somewhere on one of the endless lines in the East, the railroader rests among the repair equipment.

Summer 1944, in the days when Army Group Center collapsed, a young soldier of a crack explosion command.

July 1944, Aachen: lunch break for the train security team; in the background are two Series 57[10] freight locomotives.

July 24, 1944: a few hours before the Red Army marched into Bialystok.

Turin, August 1944: an armored division on its way to the front.

A railroad line between Antwerp and Brussels, early September 1944: a train protection platform with a captured light Flak gun, and a French locomotive in back.

Saarbruecken, August 9, 1944: on this day the 8ᵗʰ U.S. Air Fleet dropped 384 tons of bombs. In the background are locomotives of French origin.

Summer 1944: the blown-up head of a switch.

Late October 1944, between Forli and Bologna: the "Rail Wolf" in action.

October 1944: a railroad bridge
near Memel is being prepared for
exploding on the retreat.

Warsaw West, September 1944: the residents of the Polish capital on the way to the Prushkov concentration camp.

Halle on the Saale, autumn 1944: everything still seems to be running in best order. Sandwiches for mothers and children who are being moved to quarters not threatened by air raids.

Wittenberg on the Elbe, November 1, 1944: streamlining disguises an express-train locomotive of the DR, Series 01[10].

December 1944: at a depot east of the Oder, a small boy who must leave his home.

December 1944 near Allenstein: hay is transported in a French railroad wagon. The "powder flag" remains from its earlier use.

Autumn 1944: a gatekeeper.

May 1945, somewhere in Germany: though not on the "Siegfried Line," but still in front of a *Reichsbahn* freight car, two British soldiers dry their laundry.

March 1945: despite everything, someone still has a sense of humor.

Above: November 1944: a depot on the line between Csap and Tonai, Hungary, with a Series 52 war locomotive. On the stakeside car are makeshift structures for railroad Flak guns, with splinter shields. Below: between Ferrara and Padua, autumn 1944 "Scorched Earth" along the rail line.

A depot west of the Rhine in the spring of 1945: the End.

Pressburg, March 1945: a stretch of track blown up by Czech partisans.

September 12, 1944: the RAF Bomber Command dropped 1556 tons of bombs on Frankfurt on the Main.

March 1945: in a railroad tunnel north of Verona after air raids.

February 1945: British bombers attack the depot in Soltau.

Bibliography

Adler, H. G., *Der verwaltete Mensch, Studien zur Deportation der Juden aus*. Deutschland, Tuebingen 1974.

Ahlfen, H. v., Generalmajor, Der Kampf der Festung Breslau, in Wehrwissenschaftliche Rundschau, Vol. 1, 1956, Berlin-Frankfurt/Main, Der Kampf um Schlesien, Munich 1961.

Army Archives, Washington D.C.:
German Anti-Guerilla Operations in the Balkans 1941-1944, # 20-243, 1954, 82 pp.

Army Intelligence Division, Washington D.C.:
Lesson from the War, translation, registry # F-6252, 28 pp.
Resistance Factors and Special Forces Areas: Bulgaria, Project A-394, 1957, 22 pp.

Army Special Warfare Center, Fort Bragg N.C.:
Readings in Guerilla Warfare, December 1960

Augur, Die rote Partisanenbewegung. Aufbau und Kampfverfahren, Allg. Schweiz.
Militaerzeitschrift, 1949, Vol. 115, p. 441

Baedeker, Das Generalgouvernement, Leipzig 1943

Berges, Le role militaire actuel des chemins de fer, Revue de défense nationale, Paris, 1947, pp. 483-492, 666-677

Bergonzini, L., Partisanen am Monte Battaglia, Berlin 1962

Beyer, H., Dokumente ueber die faschstische Okkupation von 1939 bis 1945 in Polen, in
Wissenschaftliche Zeitschrift der Karl-Marx-Universitaet Leipzig, 1956-57, Vol. 1, pp. 11ff

Bibliographien: Buecherschau der Weltkriegsbuecherei, Bibliothek für Zeiteschichte, Stuttgart

Blindheim, S., The Strategy of Underground Warfare, Military Review, June 1951

Bork, M., Das deutsche Wehrmachttransportwesen—eine Vorstufe europaeischer Verkehrsfuehrung, in
Wehrwissenschaftliche Rundschau 2, 1952, p. 50

Bowmann, G., Strategic Bombing, London 1956

Buehler, Das Generalgouvernement, Seine Verwaltung und seine Wirtschaft. Sammlung von Vortraegen der ersten wissenschaftlichen Vortragsreihe der Verwaltungsakademie des Generalgouvernements, Krakow 1943

Bulgariens Volk im Widerstand 1941-1944, eine Dokumentation über den bewaffneten
Kampf gegen den Faschismus, Petar Georgieff & Basil Spiru, ed., Berlin 1962

Bundesarchiv Akten R43 II/184a (Reichskanzlei); R 5/125, 853, 873, 875, 589a
(Reichsverkehrsministerium), R2Zg. 1955ff; 5067, 23494, 23495, 23717, 23797
(Reichsfinanzministerium) 1E52l (Warschauer Eisenbahnen); R52 II/174-223
(Tagebuch des Generalgouvernement Dr. Frank)

Busse, H. & Dreetz, D., Neue Quellen zur Entwicklung der sowjetischen Partisanenbewegung in den Jahren 1941-42, in
Zeitschrift für Militaergeschichte, Vol. 4, pp. 91ff, Berlin 1964

Carr, E. H., German-Soviet Relations 1919-1939, London 1952
Chronik des Krieges, Dokumente und Berichte, Berlin 1940
Combaux, C., Military Activities of the French Resistance Movement, Military Review, July 1945

Dallin, Deutsche Herrschaft in Russland 1941-1945, New York/Düsseldorf 1958

Deborin, G. A., Der zweite Weltkrieg. East Berlin 1960.
Der Partisanenkampf in der Sowjetunion. Ueber Charakter, Inhalt und Formen des
Partisanenkampfes in der USSR 1941-1944, Berlin 1963

Der Prozess gegen die Hauptkriegsverbrecher vor dem Internationalen
Militsaergerichtshof in Nürnberg, 14. November 1945-11. Oktober 1946, 42 Bd., Nürnberg 1947-1949

Der Reichsführer-SS und der Chef der Deutschen Polizei: Bandenbekampfung, 1st ed.,
Sept. 1942, Reichssicherheitshauptamt, no year

Der Widerstandskämpfer (Vienna), Neue Zürcher Zeitung, 1957

Deutsche Bundesbahn, HV Dokumentationsdienst, Was geschah wann? Zahlen aus der Geschichte der Esenbahn

Deutsche Reichsbahn, Lehrstoffe für die Dienstanfaengerschule, "Bilden der Zuege", 2, new ed., Leipzig 1941.

Deutsche Reichsbahn, Reichsbahn-Zentralamt Berlin, Beschreibung der
Güterzuglokomotive Reihe 50, Berlin, no year (ca. 1938)

Die deutsche Industrie im Kriege 1939-1945, Deutscher Institut für Witrtschaftsordnung Berlin-Dahlem, Berlin 1954

Die Eisenbahn als operatives Führungsmittel, in Wehrkunde, 1953, Vol. 7, pp. 9ff

Die Gestaltung des Eisenbahnverkehrs zwischen Deutschland und der Sowjetunion im Kriege, 1940

Die kritische Transportweise im Kriege, Zeitschrift für Verkehrswissenschaft, Cologne,
26. Lg. 1955, Vol. 2, pp. 119-124

Die militaerische Bedeutung des Verkehrswesens, in Bilanz des zweiten Weltkrieges.

Die Niederlage 1945, Aus dem Kriegstagebuch des Oberkommandos der Wehrmacht,
P. E. Schramm, ed., Munich 1962

Die Ostbahn, Zeitung des Vereins Mitteleuropa, Eisenbahnverwaltungen 1941, pp. 373ff

Die Tragoedie Schlesiens 1945-46 in Dokumenten, Dr. Johannes Kaps, ed., Munich 1957

Dixon, A. & Heilbrunn, O. Partisanen, Stratu. Taktik des Guerillakrieges, Frankfurt/Main 1956

Dokumente zum Westfeldzug 1940, H. A. Jacobsen, ed., Göttingen 1960

du Prel, Das Generalgouvernement, 2nd ed., Würzburg 1942

Durrant, A. E., The Steam Locomotives of Eastern Europe, Newton Abbot 1966

Eichholtz, D., Geschichte der deutschen Kriegswirtschaft, Vol. 1, 1939-1941, East Berlin 1969

Elsners eisenbahntechnische Taschenbücher, various years 1936-1940

Ewerth, L., Der Arbeitsansatz von Landbewohnern besetzter Gebiete des Ostens und Suedostens im 2. Weltkrieg (Diss. Ms), Tuebingen 1955

Feuchter, G. W., Der Luftkrieg, 2nd ed., Geschichte des Luftkrieges, Bonn 1962

Frankland, N. & Webster, Sir Ch., The Strategic Air Offensive Against Germany 1939-1945, 4 vol., London 1961

Friedensburg, F., Sie sowjetischen Kriegslieferungen an das Hitlerreich, in Vierteljahrshefte zur Wirtschaftsforschung, Vol. 4, Berlin, 1962

Gellner, J., Partisans as a Weapon of War, The Roundel, March 1956.

German Counter-Intelligence Activities in Occupied Russia (1941-44), Office of the Chief of Military History, U.S. Department of the Army, Washington, no date

Gerteis, 5 Jahre Ostbahn (eine von dem ehemaligen Praesidenten der Generaldirektion der Ostbahn im November 1949 gefertigte und an seine Mitarbeiter verteilte Denkschrift) Organisation und Aufgaben der Ostbahn in Gegenwart und Zukunft

Geschchte des Grossen Vaterlaendischen Krieges der Sowjetunion 1941-1945 in 6 Bänden, Vol. 1-3, Berlin 1962-1964

Geschichte des zweiten Weltkrieges 1939-1945, Militaerhistorischer Abriss, unter der Redaktion von Generalmajor N. G. Pawlenko und Oberst I. W. Parotkin, 2 vol., Berlin 1961

Görlitz, W., Der zweite Weltkrieg 1939-1945, Stuttgart 1952

Gottberg, H.-L. von, Das Wesen des sowjetischen Partisanenkampfes, in Wehrkunde, Vol. 12, 1958, pp. 689ff

Gottwaldt, A. B., Deutsche Kriegslokomotiven 1939-1945, Stuttgart 1973

Government Publications:
Reichsgesetzblatt (RGBI)
Eisenbahn-Verkehrsordnung (EVO)
Eisenbahn-Bau- und Betriebsordnung (BO)
Fahrdienstvorschriften (FV)
Geschaeftsberichte der Deutschen Reichsbahn
Amts- und Nachrichtenblaetter
Erlasse, Verordnungen, Verfuegungen Vorschriften und Bekanntmachungen des Reichsverkehrsministeriums), ferner des Generaldirektors und der Hauptverwaltung
(HV) der Deutschen Reichsbahn
Sammlungen von Erlassen und Verfuegungen—
Dienstverschriften 112 und 118
Statisticshe Angaben ueber die Deutsche Reichsbahn
(Blaubuecher)

Grassmann, G. O., Die deutsche Besatzungsgesetzgebung während des zweiten Weltkrieges, Tübingen 1958

Greiner, H., Die oberste Wehrmachtführung 1939-1943, Nach dem Kriegstagebuch des Wehrmachtfuehrungsstabes, Wiesbaden 1951

Griebl, H. & Wenzel, H., Geschichte der deutschen Kriegslokomotiven, Series 42 & 52, Vienna 1971.

Gubbins, C., Resistance movements in World War II, Royal Service Institute Journal, May 1948, condensed in Military Review, January 1949

Guderian, H., Erfahrungen im Russlandkrieg, in Bilanz des zweiten Weltkrieges, p. 81ff

Guischard, Personalfürsorge dei der Ostbahn, Rechsbahn 1942

Haas, L., Auswahl und Einsatz der Ostarbeiter, Neustadt 1944

Haeseler, Erkundung und Wiederherstellung der Eisenbahnen des von der deutschen Wehrmacht besetzten Gebietes während der Kampfhandlungen, Reichsbahn 1939

Hahn, K. E., Eisenbahner in Krieg und Frieden, Farnkfurt am Main 1954

Halder, Kriegstagebuch Band 1: Vom Polenfeldzug bis zum Ende der Westoffensive 14.8.1939—30.6.1940, Stuttgart 1962

Hampe, E., Die technischen Truppen im zweiten Weltkrieg, Wehrwisenschaftliche Rundschau, 1953, pp. 509-520

Handbuch für die Dienststellen des Generalbevoooämchtigten für den Arbeitseinsatz und die interessierten Reichsstellen im Grossdeutschen Reich und in den besetzten Gebieten, F. Didier, ed, GBA, Vol. 1, Berlin 1944

Harris, A. E., Partisan Operations, Military Review, August 1950

Harris, A. T., Bomber-Offensive, London 1947

Hart, B. H. Liddell, Die Rote Armee, Bonn 1956
Die Strategie einer Diktatur, Aufstieg und Fall deutscher Generaele, Zuerich 1948

Haustein, Das Werden der Grossdeutschen Reichsbahnen im Rahmen des Grossdeutschen Reiches, Reichsbahn 1942

Hawemann, W., Achtung, Partisanen! Der Kampf hinter der Ostfront, Hannover 1953

Heelis, J. E., Guerilla Warfare and its Lessons, United Institute of India, July 1947

Heeres-Dienstvorschriften HDv:
66/3 Die Bahnhifskommandatur (Hafenoffizier), 1941
67 Wehrmacht-Eisenbahnordnung (Weo) mit dem militaerischen und den eisenbahntechnischen Ausfuehrungsbestimmungen, 1932
Zu 67 Merkheft f.d. Kriegsdauer Wehrmachttransporte auf Eisenbahnen, 1940
68/5 Heft 5, Grundsaetze für die Fahrzeugverladung auf offenen Eisenbahnwagen
und für die Errechnung des Wagenbedarfs
(Fahrzeugverladung—
Grundsaetze..F.V.Gr), 1938, 1943
68/5a Heft 5a, Ausruestung der Eisenbahnwagen für Wehrmachttransporte
(Wg.-Ausr.), 1941
68/5b Heft 5b, Anleitung zum Ein- und Ausladen mit fahrbaren Eisenbahnrampen
(Flr), 1935, 1941
68/6 Heft 6, Militaerverkehr von und nach Ostpreussen, 1937
69 Wehrmachttarif für Eisenbahnen mit

Ausführungsbestimmungen und Erlaeuterungen, 1939
69 Militaertarif für Eisenbahnen, 1936

Heilbrunn, O., Partisanenbuch, Zürich 1956

Henschel & Sohn GmbH, Kassel, Beschreibung und
Betriebsanweisung der 1'E
Henschel-Kondenslokomotive Baureihe 52 der Deutschen
Reichsbahn, Kassel 1944

Herdeg, W., Grundzüge der deutschen Besatzungsverwaltung in
den west- und nordeuropaeischen Laendern waehrend des
zweiten Weltkrieges, Studien des Instituts für
Besatzungsfragen in Tübingen, No. 1, Tübingen 1953

Heusinger, A., Befehl im Widerstreit, Schicksalsstunden der
deutschen Armee 1923-1945, Tübingen 1950

Historical Study, Russian Combat Methods in World War II, in
Department of the Army Pamphlet No. 20-230, 1950

Hitlers Weisungen für die Kriegfuehrung 1939-1945, Dokumente
des Oberkommandos der Wehrmacht, Walther Hubatsch,
ed., Frankfurt am Main, 1962

Holtz, Wieder Eisenbahnverkehr mit Russland, Zeitung des
Vereins Mitteleurop, Eisenbahnverwaltungen 1940, pp. 145ff

Ignatow, P. K., Partisanen, Berlin 1953

Jacobsen, H. A., 1939-1945, Der zweite Weltkrieg in Chronik und
Dokumenten, 4th ed., Darmstadt 1959
Jahrbuch für nationalsozialistische Wirtschaft, Berlin 1935ff

Janssen, G., Das Ministerium Speer, Berlin 1968

Joachimi, Der erste Aufbau der Eisenbahndirektion Lodz,
Reichsbahn 1939, pp. 1007ff

Kaissling, Eisenbahn-Ausbesserungswerkeim besetzten Gebiet,
Krakow 1944, Druckerei und Fahrkartenverwaltung
der Ostbahn

Kaldor, U., The German War Economy, Manchester Statistical
Society, May 2, 1946

Kehrl, H., Kriegswirtschaft und Ruestungsindustrie, in Bilanz des
zweiten Weltkrieges

Klein, B. H., Germany's Economic Preparations for War,
Cambridge MA 1959

Knuth, Vom deutschen zum grossdeutschen Reisebuero,
Grossdütscher Verkahr 1941, pp. 515ff

Koch, H. A., Flak, Bad Nauheim 1954

Körner, P., Straffste Lenkung der Kriegswirtschaft, in Der
Vierjahresplan 4, 1940

Kovpak, Generalmajor S. A., Our Partisan Course, London 1947

Kreidel, H., Partisanenkampf in Mittelrussland, in Wehrkunde,
1955, Vol. 9, pp. 380ff

Kreidler, E., Zur Problematik der Kriegsgeschichte der Deutschen
Reichsbahn im zweiten Weltkrieg, Buecherschau der
Weltkriegsbuecherei, Stuttgart, 1957
Die Eisenbahnen im Machtbereich der Achsenmaechte
während des zweiten Weltkrieges, Frankfurt am Main 1975

Kriegslok Reihe 52, Hilfsheft h 605, Leipzig 1944

Kriegstagebuch des Oberkommandos der Wehrmacht
(Wehrmachtsfuehrungsstab)
1942-1945, Vol. II-IV, ed. A. Hillgruber (1942), W. Hubatsch
(1943), P. E. Schramm (1944-45), Frankfurt am Main

Kuby,. E., Die Russen in Berlin 1945, Munich 1965

Kühnrch, H., Der Partisanenkrieg in Europa 1939-1945, Berlin
1968

Kumpf, W., Die Organisation Todt im Kriege, in Bilanz des
zweiten Weltkrieges
Der Reichsarbeitsdienst im Kriege, in Bilanz des zweiten
Weltkrieges

Küppers, H. & Barnier, R., Einsatzbedingungen der Ostarbeiter,
Berlin 1943

Landfird, W;, Die totale wirtschaftliche Mobilmachung, in Die
deutsche Volkswirtschaft

Ley, R., Die grosse Stunde, Das deutsche Volk im totalen
Kriegseinsatz, Reden und Aufsaetze 1941-1943,
Munich 1943

Lindsay, F. A., Unconventional Warfare, Foreign Affairs,
January 1962

Lippert, J., Stalingrad—ein Transportproblem (Leserzuschrift), in
Aus Politik und Zeitgeschichte, Beilage zur Wochenzeitung
"Das Parlament," No. B 20/60, May 18, 1960

Luther, H., Der franzoesische Widerstand gegen die deutsche
Besatzungsmacht und seine Bekaempfung, Studien des
Instituts für Besatzungsfragen im 2. Weltkrieg,
Tübingen 1957, No. 11

Maedel, K.-E., Die deutschen Dampflokomotiven gestern und
heute, Berlin 1965

Malinowski, W. R., The Pattern of Underground Resistance,
Annals, March 1944

Manstein, E. von, Verlorene Siege, Bonn 1955

Marshall, G. C., King, E. J. & Arnold, H. H., Der Bericht des
amerikanischen Oberkommandos, New York 1946

Metsalf, G. T., Offensive Partisan Warfare, Military Review,
April 1962

Michel, H. & Granet, M., Histoire d'un Mouvement de
Resistance, Paris 1957

Middeldorf, E., Taktik im Russlandfeldzug, Darmstadt 1956

Miksche, Lt. Col. F. O., Secret Forces, The Technique of
Underground Movements, London, 1950

Militaerwesen, Zeitschrift für Militaerpolitik, Militaertheorie und
Militaertechnik, Berlin

Military Improvisations during the Russian Campaign,
Washington, Department of the Army, 1951, 100 pp.

Milward, A. S., Die deutsche Kriegswirtschaft 1939-1945,
Schriftreihe der Vierteljahreshefte für Zeitgeschichte, No. 12,
Stuttgart 1966
Hitlers Konzept des Blitzkrieges, in Probleme des zweiten
Weltkreges, Andreas
Hillgruber, ed., Cologne 1967, pp. 19-40

Münzer, Deutsche Eisenbahner im besetzten Frankreich,
Vereinszeitung 1941, pp. 105ff

Murawski, E., Der deutsche Wehrmachtsbericht 1939 bis 1945,
2nd ed., Boppard 1962

Nardain, B., Les-Francs-Tireurs et Partisans Francais et
l'Insurrection Nationale (Juin 1940-Aout 1944), Paris 1947

Nennicke, O., Zur Zersetzung der Kampfmoral in der
faschistischen Wehrmacht, in
Militaerwesen, 1961, Vol. 9, pp. 1226ff.

Ney, V., Bibliography on Guerilla Warfare, Military Affairs,
Autumn 1960

Osanka, F. M., Der Krieg aus dem Dunkel, Cologne 1963

Österheld, A., Die deutsche Kriegswirtschaft, Leipzig 1940

Pfister, E., The Rail Transport Situation in the Caucasus 1942-1943, in Military Review, Vol. 34, No. 11, February 1955, pp. 82-86

Philippi-Heim, Der Feldzug gegen Sowjetrussland 1941-1945, Arbeitskreis für Wehrforschung, Stuttgart 1962

Picker, H., Hitlers Tischgespraeche im Fuehrerhauptquartier, Bonn 1951

Prath, Aufbauarbeit der Reichsbahndirektion Oppeln in Ostoberschlesien und im Olsagebiet, Reichsbahn 1939

Pischel, Generaldirektion der Ostbahn in Krakau 1939-1945, Archiv für Eisenbahnwesen 1964

Ploetz, Geshichte des zweiten Weltkrieges, Bielefeld 1951

Postel, C., Occupation and Resistance, abridged, Military Review, December 1948

Pottgiesser, Die Reichsbahn im Ostfeldzug, Vienna 1939-1944, 1960
    Die Deitsche Reichsbahn im Ostfeldzug 1939-1944, in Wehrmacht im Kampf, Vol. 26, Neckargemünd 1960

Railroads in Defense and War, Association of American Railroads, Washington D.C., ed. Helen Richardson

Rear Area Security in Russia, The Soviet Second Front Behind the German Lines, Washington, Department of the Army, 1951, 31 pp.

Reed, B., German Austerities, 2-10-0, in Loco-Profile 18, 1971, pp. 121-144

Redelis, V., Partisanenkrieg, Entstehung und Bekämpfung der Partisanen- und Untergrundbewegung im Mittelabschnitt der Ostfront 1941 bis 1943, Heidelberg 1958
Reichsgesetzblatt, Reichsministerium des Innern, Berlin 1933

Rezien, P., Tactics of Ambush, Field Artillery Journal, December 1942

Rhode: Das Deutsche Wehrmachtstransportwesen im zweiten Weltkrieg, Militaergeschichtliches Forschungsamt, Vol. 12, 1971

Rhode, G., Die Ostgebiete des Deutschen Reiches, Würzburg

Richardson, H. R., Railroads in Defense and War, A Bibliography, Washington 1953
    Richtlinien es Oberkommandos der Wehrmacht für die Bandenbekaempfung vom 6. Mai 1944

Rigg, R. B., The Guerilla—a Factor in War, Army Cavalry Journal, Nov.-Dec. 1949

Roos, G., Die deutschen Bautruppen im zweiten Weltkrieg, in Wehrw. Rdsch. 4, 1954

Rossi, A., The Russo-German Alliance 1939-1941, London 1950
    Zwei Jahre deutsch-sowjetisches Buendnis, 1954

Rostow, W. W., Guerilla Warfare in Underdeveloped Areas, Marine Corps Gazette, Special Guerilla Warfare Issue, January 1962

Rumpf,. H., De Industrie im Bombenkrieg, in Wehrw. Rdsch. 3, 1953

arter, Landesverteidigung und Eisenbahn, Gerstenberg 1955

asse, Die deutsche Signaltechnik im zweiten Weltkrieg, 1958

chaper, Zerstörung und Wiederherstellung von Eisenbahnbruecken und Tunneln im ehemaligan Polen, Zeitung Verein Mittelurop. Esenbahnverwaltungen, 1939

chlichting, Grossdeutschlands Spediteurgewerbe—Das Bindeglied zwischen Verkehr und Wirtschaft, Grossdeutscher Verkehr 1941

Schmidt-Richberg, E., Die Deutsche Reichsbahn im Ostfeldzug 1939-1944, in Wehrmacht im Kampf, Vol. 26, Neckargemünd 1960

Schneider, E., Technik und Waffenentwicklung im Kriege, in Bilanz des zweiten Weltkrieges.

Schnez, A., Luftjkrieg ohne Terrorangriffe, Studie über den Kampf "Transportsysteme", Wehrw. Rdsch, 1952, pp. 275-281

Schoenleben, E., Fritz Todt—Der Mensch der Ingenieur, der Nationalsozialist, Oldenburg 1943

Schuchmann, Deutsche Fronteisenbahner zwischen Westwall unf Maginot-Linie, Reichsbahn 1941, Vol. 1, pp. 4ff

Schultz, J., Die letzten dreissig Tage, Stuttgart 1951

Schwarze, J et al., Die Dampflokomotive, Berlin 1965

Scotland, R., Die Rueckwirkungen der Kriegszerstoerungen und der Betriebseinschraenkungen auf den Verkehr der Deutschen Reichsbahn in den Jahren 1945 bis 1946, Hannover (Dissertation, Technische Hochschule)

Seidl, Die Beziehungen zwischen Deuitschland und der Sowjetunion 1939-1941, Dokumente des Auswaertigen Amtes, Tübingen 1949

Seversky, SA., Entscheidung durch Luftmacht, Stuttgart 1951

Slezak, j. O., Breite Spur und weite Strecken, Transpress-Verlag, Berlin 1963

Sommerlatte, Verkehrsleistungen der Deutschen Reichsbahn im Kriege, Zeitung Mitteleurop. Eisenbahnbverwaltungen 1941, pp. 143ff

Speer, A., Die Vergrösserung der Produktion, in Das Reich, 1942 Erinnerungen, Berlin 1969

Statistisches Jahrbuch für das Deutsche Reich 1941-42, Berlin 1942

Stocklausner, H., 25 Jahre deutsche Einheitslokomotiven, Nürnberg 1950

Strausz-Hupe, R., Soviet Psychological Strategy, U.S. Naval Institute Proceedings, June 1961

Tanham, G. K., The Belgium Underground Movement 1940-1944, Stanford CA, Stanford University 1951 (unpublished PhD Dissertation)

Teske, H., Die militaerische Bedeutung des Verkahrswesens, in Bilanz des zweiten Weltkrieges, pp. 299-310, Oldenburg 1953.
    Die silbernen Spiegel, Generalstabsdienst unter der Lupe, Heidelberg 1952
    Der Wert von Eisenbahnbruecken, Wehrwissenschaftliche Rundschau, 1954, pp. 514-523
    Partisanen gegen die Eisenbahnen, in Wehrw. Rdsch. 1953, Vol. 10, pp. 468ff

Thomas, G., Geschichte der deutschen Wehr- und Rüstungswirtschaft (1919-1944/45), W. Birkenfeld, ed., Boppard am Rhein 1966

Tippelskirch, K. von, Geschichte des zweiten Weltkrieges, Bonn 1951

Tito, I. B., The Yugoslavian Army, Military Review, September 1945

Townsend, E. C., Esponage, Underground Forces and Guerillas, Fort Leavenworth KS, 1946

Vereinigung deutscher Lokomotivfabriken , Die deutsche Lokomotiv-Industrie im zweiten Weltkrieg (ed. Steinhauser), Frankfurt am Main 1959

Verzeichnis der höheren Reichsbahnbeamten 1943, verschiedene Merkbuecher für Schienenfahrzeuge der DRB, amtliche Unterlagen der dRB

Wagenführ, R., Die deutsche Industrie im Krieg 1939-1945, Berlin 1963

Watzdorf, B., Vorbereitunger der faschistischen Wehrmacht auf dem Gebiet des Transportwesens für den Überfall auf Polen, in Zeitschrift für Militaergeschichte, Vol. 3, No. 1, Berlin 1964.

Webster, C. & Frankland, N., The Strategic Air Offensive Against Germany 1939-1945, 3 vol., London 1961

Welter, E., Falsch und richtig planen, Eine kritische Studie über die deutsche Wirtschaftslenkung im zweiten Weltkrieg, Forschungsinstitut für Wirtschaftspolitik an der Universitaet Mainz, Vol. 1, Heidelberg 1954

Wehde-Textor, O., Archiv für Eisenbahnwesen, 71st Year, Die Leistungen der Deutschen Reichsbahn im zweiten Weltkrieg, 1961

Wehner, H., Der Einsatz der Esenbahnen dür die verbrecherischen Ziele des faschistischen deutschen Imperialismus im 2. Weltkrieg, Dresden (Dissertation, Hochschule für Verkehrswesen) 1961

Wiens, Kämpferischer Ensatz der Fronteisenbahner beim Aufstand in Warschau, Reichsbahn 1944
Bericht über die Räumung des Restbezirks der Ostbahndirektion Warschau

Wilmot, Ch., Der Kampf um Europa von Duenkirchen bis Berlin, 2nd ed., Frankfurt 1960

Windisch, Die deutsche Nachschubtruppe im zweiten Weltkrieg, 1953

Winkler, K., Die Partisanenkriegführung, Dissertation, Mainz 1953 (manuscript)

Wirtschaft und Statistik, Statistisches Reichsamt, Berlin 1939ff

Witte, F., Die Entwicklung der 1E-h2 Kriegslokomotive Reihe 52 der Deutschen Reichsbahn (Denkschrift der DRB), Berlin 1942
Zehn Jahre Reichsbahn-Zentralamt und die Kriegslokomotiven 1935-1945, in Lokmagazin 40, 1970

Wittekind, K., Aus 20 Jahren deutscher Wehrwirtschaft 1925-1945, in Wehrkunde 6, 1957

Wolters, R., Albert Speer, Oldenburg 1943

Wozniesienski, N., Wojennaja Ekonomika ZSSR, Moscow 1948

Wrzosek, M., Znaaczenie Kolei Generalnego Gubernatorstwa dla dzialan wojennych na woshodzie i ich ochrona przez niemieckie sily okupacyjne, in 20 Lat Ludowego Wojska Polskiego, Warsaw 1967

Ziel, R., Raeder müssen rollen, Stuttgart 1973

Periodicals:

Eisenbahn, Vienna, various years

Eisenbahn-Kurier, Solingen, various years

Energie, Technische Fachzeitschrift der DAF, Berlin, 1942

Die Lokomotive, Vienna and Bielefeld, 1939

Schienenverkehr, Vienna, various years

Werksnachrichten der WLF, Vienna, 1941 to 1944

Zeitung des Vereins Mitteleurop. Eisenbahnverwaltungen (Organization Journal)

Organ für die Fortschritte des Eisenbahnwesens, Archiv für Esenbahnwesen

Zeitschrift für das gesamte Eisenbahn-Scherungs- und Fernmeldewesen

Zeitschrift des Internationalen Eisenbahnverbandes UIC Eisenbahnfachmann

A Word of Thanks

I would like to express my hearty thanks for their friendly assistance to:

Dr. M. Haupt and his colleagues, Federal Archives, Koblenz.

All the staff of the Photographic Library, imperial War Museum, London.

Mr. J. S. Lucas and Mr. P. H. Reed, Imperial War Museum, London.

Captain J. Wronski, Capt. W. Milewski, Capt. H. Dembinski, Capt. S. Zurakowski, Sikorski Institute, London.

Dr. von Gersdorff and Dr. Fricke, Militaergeschichtliches Forschungsamt, Freiburg.

Mr. M. Meyer, Militaerarchiv, Freiburg.

Dr. M. Lindemann, Institut für Zeitungsforschung, Dortmund.

Prof. Dr. J. Rohwer, Mr. Haupt and their colleagues, Bibliothek für Zeitschchichte, Stuttgart.

Dr. Sack and his colleagues, Zentralbibliothek der Bundeswehr, Düsseldorf.

Ms. Stöhr and Ms. Traexler, Bücherei der Bundesbahndirektion, Munich.

Mr. Keller, Hauptverwaltung der Deutschen Bundesbahn, Frankfurt/M.

Mr. Pfeiffer, Dokumentationsdienst der Deutschen Bundesbahn, Frankfurt/M.

Pressedienst, Bundesbahn-Zentralamt, Munich.

Mr. Illeseer, Verkehrsarchiv beim Zentralmuseum, Nürnberg.

Mr. Sembritzki, Blohm & Voss, Hamburg

Mr. Glomp, Krauss-Maffei, Munich.

Mr. Osterwald, Krupp Industrie und Stahlbau, Esen.

Dr. Flier, MaK, Kiel—Munich.

Mr. Wolf, MAN-Werk, Nürnberg.

Mr. Noack, Orenstein & Koppel, Dortmund-Dorstfeld.

Mr. Schmidt, Thyssen Henschel, Kassel.

Mr. F. Englberger, Bundbahnoberamt, Retired, Munich.

Mr. H. Wenzel, Koblenz-Metternich.

Mr. S. Horn, Motorbuch-Verlag, Stuttgart.

Photo Credits:

Federal Archives, Koblenz

Imperial War Museum, London

Établissement Cinématographique et Photographique des Armées, Fort d'Ivry

The Library of Congress, Washington D.C.

Archives of M. R. de Launay, Paris

Archives of J. S. Middleton, London

Archives of J. K. Piekalkiewicz

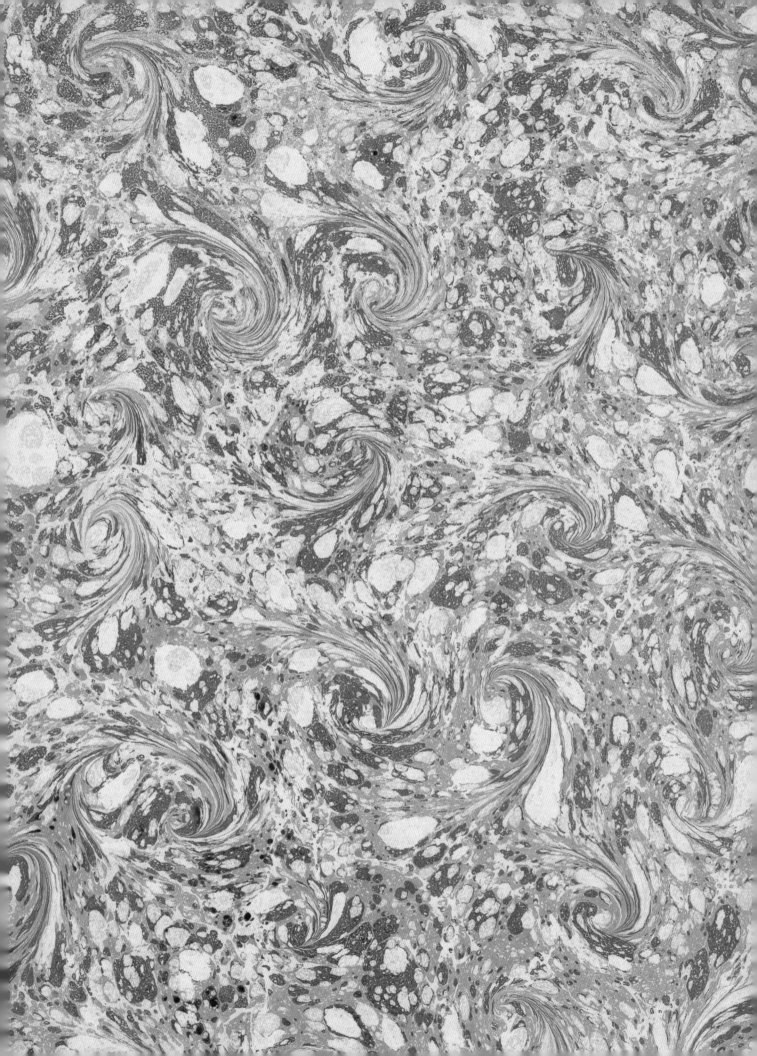